DAILY WE FOLLOW HIM

Learning Discipleship from Peter

by

M. Basil Pennington, O.C.S.O.

Complete and Unabridged
Originally published as *In Peter's Footsteps*

IMAGE BOOKS
A Division of Doubleday & Company, Inc.
Garden City, New York
1987

Image Books Edition published February 1987 by special
arrangement with Doubleday & Company, Inc.

Library of Congress Cataloging-in-Publication Data

Pennington, M. Basil.
Daily we follow him.

Originally published under title: In Peter's footsteps.
1. Peter, the Apostle, Saint. 2. Bible. N.T.
Peter—Criticism, interpretation, etc. 3. Christian life—
Catholic authors. I. Title.
[BS2515.P455 1987]   225.9′24   86–20157
ISBN 0–385–23535-6 (pbk.)

DAILY WE FOLLOW HIM

To Paul
and all the other members of
Alcoholics Anonymous
– a constant source of inspiration –
with gratitude

Contents

Contents

Forward

Christ is our master and we are his disciples. This is our great privilege.

My monastery at Spencer has been blessed with very special neighbors. Off to the west we have a Buddhist meditation center, and to the south there is a Hindu ashram. There is an excellent rapport among us; we partake of each other's joys and sorrows. We realize we are all seekers, and share a common concern for the uplifting and healing of this world of ours. Our lives exemplify many common values. One of these is discipleship. Our Buddhist and Hindu brothers and sisters have an almost unbounded enthusiasm for their masters. There is no doubt they consider it a great privilege to be disciples. They are tireless in extolling their teacher of meditation. When Achincha comes from Thailand, our Buddhist brethren rise to new levels of excitement. They are eager for us to come to their center to see and hear him; they want to bring him to speak to us at our monastery. And the same is true in regard to Swamiji. In all of this, I cannot help reflecting on our relative lack of enthusiasm and pride in regard to our Master—and he is the Master who made these others masters!

One of the things a disciple needs to learn from a

master is how to be a good disciple. In this regard we could not have a better master than our Lord Jesus. He always did the things that pleased the Father, being obedient unto death, even death on a cross. His meat was to do the will of him who sent him. His whole life and being strained to fulfill the mission he had been given. He set his face resolutely toward Jerusalem. He wept at its unresponsiveness. And he died. "Not my will but yours be done, Father."

Through a filial relationship Jesus brought a new dimension to discipleship. There was, along with a total dedication to the glorification of his Master-Father, a deep love for the Father, a most intimate communion. And he has called us to this same kind of relationship as disciples: I shall not call you servants anymore, because a servant does not know his master's business; I call you friends because I have made known to you everything I have learned from my Father (John 15:15). He prayed that we would be one with him even as he is one with the Father (John 17:21). In baptism, through the power of his cross, he effects this essentially. It is our life's work to learn to think and act in accord with who we are by creation and by the recreation of baptism.

But Jesus' example of discipleship can be overwhelming for us. He *always* did the things that pleased the Father. How often we fail!

This is where Saint Peter comes in. I give him his title of "saint" quite deliberately here. For I suspect when I propose calling Peter a "master of discipleship," you might have some serious reservations. Rather quickly there comes to mind our Lord's stinging rebuke to this overzealous follower: "Get behind me, Satan!

You are an obstacle in my path . . ." Or that much more prophetic statement: "Before the cock crows twice, you will have disowned me three times." Even now, this blustery man's oaths that he does not even know the Master sting our hearts. Well might he cry, sob inconsolably—the traitor! Yet it is precisely because Peter—Saint Peter—was such a disciple, one who would fail, and fail miserably, that he is a good master of discipleship for us. Because we too fail. In the end he died for his Master, and greater love than this no man hath, than he lay down his life for his Friend and Master.

We fail. How many times! And we are, in the face of our many failures, tempted to become discouraged, to feel that we can never be true disciples of Christ. We begin to reconcile ourselves to being some kind of borderline Christian, one who will, by God's mercy, somehow slip into the outer reaches of heaven. He heard the dying thief; we can hope he will hear us when we cry out from our deathbeds. But for us there is no hope of being a true disciple. We have all our passions and emotions. We are men and women of the world with family and business to preoccupy us. We even have mothers-in-law to challenge to their very core whatever patience and love we do have. We can't leave all things to follow on the high adventure of discipleship.

Or can we?

I would like to invite you to walk with me awhile along the roads and in the towns and villages of Galilee and Judaea and watch another man—very much a man, a man of flesh and blood, of passion and emotion—as he tries to enter into the way of a disciple. We will watch and listen, and talk about it a bit as we reflect together. In the end, maybe we will let our imaginations carry us to Rome and see a man who has finally learned that God's thoughts are not our thoughts nor his ways our ways as he hangs upside down and sees all creation hanging on the mercy of God.

I must confess I am feeling a bit—or more than a bit —excited as we start out on this journey together. Maybe I am finding something of the enthusiasm of my Buddhist and Hindu neighbors. Come and see and hear our master—a master of discipleship, who will show us how to be true disciples of the one Lord and Master who is God, over all, forever and ever. May he be blessed!

We are certainly blessed ourselves in being called with Peter to be Jesus' disciples, disciples who are called not servants but friends, called to the deepest, most loving, and most fulfilling union. "Peter, do you love me?" "Yes, Lord, you know that I love you." It is, in sum, a way of love that leads not only to perfect love ("No greater love than this . . ."), but to an eternal dwelling place and unending glory: "Father, I want those you have given me to be with me where I am, so that they may always see the glory you have given me because you loved me from the foundation of the world" (John 17:24). "Those who prove victorious I will allow to share my throne, just as I was victorious myself and took my place with my Father on his throne" (Revelation 3:21).

To this, Peter was called. This is something important to remember. It was Jesus who chose Peter: "I have chosen you, you have not chosen me"—and *with* (he

didn't leave them behind—at least, not right away) all
his faults and failures and human weakness. Peter followed. We too are called. And we too can follow, even
with all our faults and failures and weakness. (Who was
that saint who for years prayed: "Lord, give me chastity,
but not yet"?—the great Saint Augustine!) We can be
confident that in the end, that love which is greater
than love, *mercy,* will win out. And we too will see and
accept the true being of things—even if it turns our
world upside down—and know that greatest joy of any
true disciple: to be with our Master, no longer serving
from afar, but rejoicing in a most complete oneness of
consummate love.

This book is meant to be an experience in shared
lectio. Lectio is an essential element in the monastic life.
If you look at the old *horaria* or timetables for the
monks' day, you find many periods simply marked *lectio.* It was a time when the monk would sit down with
the Word of God and enter into a whole process: *lectio,
meditatio, oratio, contemplatio. Lectio,* which literally
means reading, is receiving the Revelation through
reading the Sacred Scriptures or recalling what has
been previously read or heard. *Meditatio* is the process
whereby what we have received is interiorized to form
our minds and hearts. *Oratio* is our response to this.
God has spoken to us. We have heard. We now respond
to him. In *contemplatio* our response, rather than some
specific words or thoughts or affections, is the response
of our whole being in silent presence to God. Contemplation is the consummation of the process, but it does
not necessarily have to stop there. As Saint Bernard
taught, there is another step, where we go on to share

the fruit of our contemplation with others: *contemplationem aliis tradere.* Some of the richest spiritual literature available to us is precisely this, the sharing of the fruit of contemplation of the Fathers and Mothers who have gone before us.

In the rabbinical tradition it is said that Scripture is a *PaRDeS,* which means an orchard. It is full of fruit. *P* stands for *peshat,* the simple, literal meaning of the word. *R, remeg,* is that meaning which is hinted at, the allegorical, the concealed meaning that fills out our experience of the reality something like a dream arising from the lower regions of our consciousness. *Drash, D,* is the searched-out, learned interpretation. And *sod, S,* is the secret, mystical, universal meaning, the transpersonal, the meaning that is hidden in God. In the Christian tradition we find a similar approach to the Sacred Word. Medieval exegesis spoke of four meanings: the literal, the allegorical, the moral, and the anagogical. The first two would be very much the same as in the rabbinical tradition. The moral meaning refers to the response that the Revelation calls forth from us and in us. The anagogical points to the ultimate meaning; it is not unlike *sod.* As we listen to the Scriptures we can be open to all these meanings, seek them out, and let them speak to us.

The Scriptural Texts represent not only the consciousness of the original writer but also, or rather, the collective consciousness of the Christian community. Under the Divine Inspiration he was a mouthpiece of the community *that goes on* in salvation history. We are invited to enter into this consciousness of the living Body of Christ.

We have been baptized into Christ, therefore we are all called to be disciples, friends, lovers, one with Christ in a participation of being and nature beyond anything we can comprehend. In order to be integral, to be true to who we are as men and women baptized into Christ, we must also have the mind of Christ: "Let this mind be in you which was in Christ Jesus." An awesome call! We look for examples among the disciples who were schooled by Christ himself. John the Beloved, the disciple whom Jesus loved, is perhaps the most attractive. But his way is one of intuitive love. It is more to be followed than studied. It can only be learned by experience. Peter, on the other hand, is a wonderfully human fellow who seems a lot closer to us—a good place for us to start to learn to be disciples. The Scriptures are full of information about this disciple of the Lord from the day of his call till, as a wise old shepherd, he shares his heart's concerns with all of us disciples of Christ. The sacred writers do not aim so much to set forth a factual historical record as to present a true image of the person in his precise role in Salvation History. The events recorded by the Evangelists concerning Peter were chosen precisely for the same reason I am writing: to present Peter as disciple and apostolic leader.

As we come into contact with Peter, we really want to open ourselves to the experience: to listen to our own emotions, our own present experiences, to all the components of the scene. We want to note the details and the oddities. We want to allow embarrassment to rise up in us, and also dread. All our associations are relevant. We want to take responsibility, for we have a role in creating the experience. We want to face the demands of the dialectic, allowing opposites to come together. We dare to look at our many selves and ask of each character, why do we create it this way. We want to look at the origins, the unity, and the "now." You are Peter. I am Peter. Each character is you and I. The Body of Christ is a hologram. The whole is in every member. The whole of discipleship is in Peter, in you and in me in potency. It is a question of letting it come forth. We can facilitate this by touching ourselves in Peter. (The word "touching" means to experience something very concretely, incarnationally, in body and soul at the same time.) What Peter once did is also for us to do in our own proper way, the bad as well as the good—for failure is a way to repentance, self-knowledge, growth, and greater intimacy. True, we do want to get to know ourselves, to tell ourselves about ourselves. But we are also afraid. We can only move with our own ability to endure awareness, while at the same time seeking to enlarge that ability. That is why we need to pray for courage when we read Sacred Scripture or a commentary such as this, which is a shared experience of Scripture.

Sacred Scripture, the Revelation, is not something static. Is is a living Word, it is constantly in motion. Like the whole of creation, it is ever coming forth from God, coming forth now in the collective memory of a people. It is coming forth to us, it is coming forth in us, now. It is a new (re-newed) reality, and yet it is the same reality present now. The same, yet wholly new. How will I live it now, today?

I have included the texts of most of the pericopes on Peter to encourage you to enter into them yourself. Under the Holy Spirit, allow them to become your own experience. Enjoy Peter to the full, and fill in the gaps out of your own experience of discipleship.

This chapter is entitled "Forward," not "Foreword." Let us go forward together on the exciting journey of discipleship.

Father Basil
Feast of the Holy Transfiguration, 1984

Called

As John stood there with two of his disciples, Jesus passed, and John stared hard at him and said, "Look, there is the lamb of God." Hearing this, the two disciples followed Jesus. Jesus turned round, saw them following and said, "What do you want?" They answered, "Rabbi"—which means Teacher—"where do you live?" "Come and see," he replied; so they went and saw where he lived, and stayed with him the rest of that day. It was about the tenth hour.

One of these two who became followers of Jesus after hearing what John had said was Andrew, the brother of Simon Peter. Early next morning, Andrew met his brother and said to him, "We have found the Messiah"—which means the Christ— and he took Simon to Jesus. Jesus looked hard at him and said, "You are Simon son of John; you are to be called Cephas"—meaning Rock. [John 1:35–42]

We tend to think that our own lives and our own times are absolutely unique, that no one before has ever been through the things we are going through. But we are all cut out of the same human fabric, we are all part of the whole. One of the fruits of friendship, indeed one of its causes, is that kind of open sharing in which we discover that another is experiencing the very same things that we are. As wise old Solomon said, there is nothing new under the sun.

In recent years we have seen the phenomenon of many young people, and some not so young, heading east, going on a great pilgrimage to find a spiritual master—a guru, a swami, a teacher—one who has found the meaning of life and is willing to teach in a practical way how others can find that same meaning. This pilgrimage to the East in search of a master is nothing new. Back in the fourth century my own blessed patron, Basil, and his friend Gregory Nazianzus left the lecture halls of Athens to search for true wisdom in the East. From Rome the young Dalmatian, John Cassian, did the same. There were many others. And there were women too: Paula, Melenia the Elder, and Melenia the Younger, to mention only a few of the better known. At that time the East meant Syria, Palestine, and Egypt. The same phenomenon was seen in the eleventh and twelfth centuries. As we read the Gospels we find a similar quest going on in our Lord's time. John and Andrew, and Peter also, had left the lakeside of Galilee and had traveled south and east to beyond the Jordan in search of someone who seemed to have some prophetic wisdom, who seemed to have a word of life that could stir up their faith and give more meaning to their lives. They went in search of a seemingly strange man who came from the desert, wearing camel's hair, an ascetic who had a prophetic word. There was courage here, an openness, a questing, a searching. These men wanted a master; they wanted a teacher, a leader. They humbly realized that they didn't have all the answers. They wanted more, and they had the courage to go out and seek it.

God has a profound reverence for us. He knows that the greatest thing he has given us is our freedom, for therein lies our power to love. He will never violate that freedom. He will not invade our lives unless we invite him in. "Ask and you shall receive, seek and you shall find." If we want the Lord to be the master of our lives, we must seek him, invite him.

These young men from Galilee were seeking, were looking for a true master. And they were not disappointed. As John and Andrew stood beside John the Baptizer on the banks of the Jordan, suddenly the prophet raised his arm, and with shining eyes he pointed beyond the crowd to a more distant figure: "Look! Look! There is the Lamb of God." John and Andrew heard that prophetic word and quickly they went in pursuit.

Jesus became aware of his followers. He turned and asked them, "What are you looking for? What do you want?" It is the same question he constantly asks each one of us. He will give us whatever we really want. These young searchers knew what they wanted. They wanted a teacher, and they wanted to stay with him to learn the way of life. So they answered, "Rabbi [which means teacher], where do you live?" Jesus generously responded, "Come and see." So they went and saw where he lived, and they stayed with him the rest of the day. It was already toward evening.

John goes on to tell us that these two, he and Andrew, became at that moment followers of Jesus. Early the next morning, filled with the enthusiasm of a new disciple, Andrew went to his brother Simon: "We have found the Messiah," the Christ, the Anointed One, the great Teacher. Peter too was a seeker, or he would not have been there with his brother and with his co-laborer, John. We do not know exactly what the term Messiah meant to Andrew and Peter at that point. The expectation at that time, especially among the Galileans, was for a Messiah who would not only renew the religious life of the Jewish people, but would lead them to throw off the yoke of the mighty Romans—an anti-Roman nationalist leader was what was generally wanted. Such expectations were certainly very different from those of their newly found Master. Unfortunately, even today we find among those who profess to be followers of Christ, the Prince of Peace, some who think in military terms and would impose their ideas of morality, partial and degraded though they sometimes be, by means of law and military might. Whatever their image of the Messiah might have been, however distorted, the fact is that the disciples came to the Master to learn, to grow, to undergo a transformation of consciousness. We will see a long and sometimes painful process taking place as Peter little by little comes to a true understanding of the meaning of "Messiah," and what that entails in his own life as a disciple who accepts the Messiah in the true sense. For now Peter is open to learn and grow, and that is enough for the Master. It is a starting place. Peter will not be long with Christ before he sees Christ's first sign, the changing of water into wine. Perhaps this miracle was meant to indicate to Peter the transformation that must take place in him and in his thinking before he will be able to serve the Lord effectively and bring joy into the celebration of life.

The way in which Peter was initially called to discipleship tells us something about him. We see constantly in the Gospels that Peter is by nature a leader. It is quite logical to suppose that Andrew is his younger rather than his older brother; Andrew readily accepts his leadership. Yet on this occasion Peter accepts his younger brother's lead and witness. He follows, and he finds. There must be a humble openness in us who would become disciples, a willingness to listen and to follow others who have discovered something, even those who are not naturally leaders, even when we ourselves are natural leaders. True disciples are open to the Master revealing himself through anyone, through any situation, any circumstance. There is such a longing to find the Master, to find the truth, the way of life, that there is openness even to one's younger brother!

For most of us, the call does not come through great visions. There will not be angels coming down to us as to the shepherds, or Gabriel to Mary. There will not be a saint to come to us as Bridget came to Joan of Arc. There will rather be some very familiar person who will perhaps share with us something of his own vision. It can be our own brother, even our "kid brother." How often do we hold back because the call comes through someone we know only too well. This ordinary guy who is just like us, this backslider whom we know only too well, or this person who is anything but a model of virtue, suddenly gets religion and is all enthused. And our tendency? To resent rather than rejoice in his new-found meaning of life. We tend rather to reject than accept and join with him. Peter had the courage to follow this younger brother in his enthusiasm, and thus he discovered for himself that Jesus is indeed the Messiah, the Master, the Hope of Israel.

Peter followed Andrew, who took him to Jesus. John tells us that Jesus "looked hard" at Peter. Simon had leadership qualities. He was a man who was born to lead. And it would take someone who was an even greater leader to call him forth as a disciple. Jesus knew Peter's metal. So he looked hard at him. He looked deeply into him. He spoke to the depths of Peter's soul; he saw the quality, the quality that he, his Creator, had put there, and he spoke to it. "You are Simon son of John; you are to be called Cephas." Saint John tells us that this new name means rock. There are times in the history of Peter when it seems that this was almost an ironical name that Jesus gave to this floundering, fumbling man. Yet the day would come when Jesus would explain to him what his name "Rock" really meant, and then give him the grace and the power to live that meaning to the full. But for the moment it was a significant calling, a moment of profound conversion.

As Jesus looked at Peter, Peter knew that Jesus knew him to his very depths. So he was not at all surprised when Jesus addressed him by name: "You are Simon son of John." Nor, probably, was he surprised that the Master gave him a new name. Peter sensed a turning point in his life. He knew that he was no longer simply Simon son of John. He was now Peter, the disciple of Jesus the Christ.

In the Christian community it has long been the

practice at the moment when one first formally becomes a disciple of Jesus to receive a new name. In
Christian monasticism it also has been the practice—
and still is, though it is waning somewhat in some of
our western monasteries—to give the young man or the
young woman entering upon the monastic life a new
name, for monastic profession is seen as a "second baptism." The practice is waning because we no longer
have many true spiritual fathers or spiritual mothers
with the prophetic insight to see in the person coming
to the monastic life something of what he is called to, so
as to give him a name that bespeaks his calling. Parents,
in choosing a name for their child who is to be baptized
into Christ, should try to reflect deeply in prayer and
give a name that will really express in some way the call
of their child to be a follower of Jesus and to live a
Christian life. Usually it is a question of giving the child
a heavenly patron, someone who expresses the fullness
of the Christ life and can be a model. If parents truly
seek in prayer, they can count on the Holy Spirit to
inspire them in the choice of an appropriate patron.

Peter had a new name. It would be a long time before he would really be able to live up to it. As we enter
into the discipleship of Christ, the call is to something
immensely great, something that is far beyond us; it is a
call to a new level of being. It will in fact be a lifetime's
labor to come to what we are called to be. We can take
heart in walking with Peter, seeing his struggles, his
falls, and his rising again. And know that we too can
struggle, fall, and rise, and still be disciples of Jesus, and
still harbor the hope that in the end we will come to live
up to the fullness of that to which we are called.

One of the real struggles of life is this: At some moment—and it is usually at a moment like the one Andrew, John, and Peter are just experiencing, a moment of calling—we perceive an ideal, a vision, something that is big enough to call us forth in all our fullness. It is exciting. It is the sort of thing that leads men and women into monasteries, into missions, into launching a whole new career—a vision of their lives making a difference. And then soon enough our feet are back on earth. We are face to face with the daily, everyday life, with reality in all its drabness and all its shoddiness. A young man enters the monastery, and soon finds that those monks who looked so holy from the visitors' chapel are really very human beings, with the same sort of weaknesses and failures as everyone else. Monks get angry, they can be selfish, they can have bad days, and so on. A marriage partner who used to melt our heart doesn't look so enchanting rolling out of bed in the morning, especially after a bad night. Herein lies the challenge.

There seem to be three possibilities. We can cling to the ideal and refuse to accept the real, spending our lives ever seeking the ideal—the ideal teacher, the ideal place, the ideal circumstances. One day I sat in on an interesting dialogue between two well-known spiritual masters of our times. One of them was a great swami from the East. He had brought the depth of his tradition to America and had used it to open the way for many young Americans. He himself was most faithful in his everyday practice of the tradition that he taught. The other master was a very popular teacher, a Westerner who had adopted Eastern style. He had gone to

India and found a teacher there. But he continued on in a tireless quest, seeking to draw from this master and that, willing to experiment with everything he found, always looking for that teacher, that situation, that practice which would finally bring him to a wholly new level of being. The wise swami from Sri Lanka said to him, If a man keeps starting to dig a well and after a few feet stops and goes to start in another place, he will never reach the deep resources that lie far beneath the surface. One must stay in one place and dig and dig and dig. One must be faithful to an ideal and to a practice.

Another alternative that we can choose is to let go of the ideal and be "realistic," accept the seemingly real and settle down in it. The end of this can be totally frustrating, as it is going nowhere. It may be easy to glide with it for a time. But sooner or later we realize that it is a dead end.

The third alternative is to hold fast to the ideal but lovingly embrace the real and live with that life-giving tension which involves constantly trying to bring the real to the ideal.

In his call to discipleship, Peter saw the ideal in Jesus the Master. And Peter's own particular expression of that ideal was prophetically revealed to him in the new name he received: Cephas, Peter, Rock. But he still had to live with and learn to accept the real Simon, the blustery fisherman from the shores of the Lake of Galilee, who was ambitious, who was blunt and overly forthright, insensitive, and cowardly. He had to get to know himself, accept himself, and then, by his Master's teaching and grace, go beyond himself.

On this day John, Andrew, and Peter became disciples. Quickly others joined them. As disciples of Christ, life still had to go on. They had to return to their boats and their nets and earn their daily bread, take care of their families, and fulfill their social obligations. But as they went back to the shores of the Sea of Galilee, everything had new meaning. The openness, the searching that had brought them to the eastern side of Jordan remained. There was a new openness to the potential in life. There was a new openness to the Master, the Teacher, who would help them discover the full meaning of their lives. They came back to their work, their families, their friends with a certain spirit of detachment. They knew that catching fish, and making money, and enjoying friends, and fulfilling their daily tasks were not the ultimate meaning of life. There grew in their hearts a disposition that would enable them to hear God call them to something more, would enable them in part or in full to let go of these ordinary, everyday values of life for something that was more valuable. For some of the disciples of Jesus, life would continue very much as before in its outward circumstances, but there would be a new, deeper meaning, a new freedom, a new joy. There would be more time set aside for reading the Scriptures and for praying. There would be days set aside when they would go off to listen to the Master. There would be a new leaven in their lives. For others, there would come the day when they would be called to lay aside the ordinary values of life in order to follow Jesus in a special way.

This brief pericope on the first call of Peter doesn't really tell us very much about him. In fact, he probably knew very little about himself at this point, but that self-knowledge would grow. Most of us do not know too much about ourselves when we are first called. If our first call came at infant baptism, this is quite obvious. But this was probably true even if it came later in life.

I think of one of the best-known converts in our Catholic community today, Thomas Merton. As a young man he was always a searcher, looking for ultimate meaning in life. He was wholehearted in his search, whether it meant seeking that ultimate meaning in the pleasures of the world, in drink and in sex, or in social concern—he was even a card-carrying Communist—or in listening to an Indian swami. In the end he did find ultimate meaning in the Catholic faith. And he entered wholeheartedly into that faith. He became a monk. Yet even as a monk, at first he didn't have it all put together. He didn't know the true value of God's world, nor even of his own self. He was fortunately blessed with a very wise Father Abbot. Dom Frederic Dunne first made him write his own autobiography so that he could reclaim all the energies, the searching, the desire for life. Merton was then put to teaching—the best way to learn anything is to teach—the patristic heritage. As Merton—or Father Louis, as he was called in the monastery of Gethsemani—studied the Greek Fathers, he discovered a reality of which these Fathers were very much aware. God isn't just to be found in *theoria*—contemplation—of the beyond. God is very present in his creation. They spoke of *theoria physica,* of the presence of God the Word in his creation, of the *logoi.* This all came together for Merton through the experience of a dream that came to life for him a few days later. In a very exceptional letter to Boris Pasternak he tells us about it:

It is a simple enough story but obviously I do not tell it to people—you are the fourth who knows it, and there seems to be no point in a false discreteness that might restrain me from telling you since it is clear that we have so very much in common.

One night I dreamt that I was sitting with a very young Jewish girl of fourteen or fifteen, and that she suddenly manifested a very deep and pure affection for me and embraced me so that I was moved to the depths of my soul. I learned that her name was "Proverb," which I thought very simple and beautiful. And also I thought: "She is of the race of Saint Anne." I spoke to her of her name, and she did not seem to be proud of it, because it seemed that the other young girls mocked her for it. But I told her that it was a very beautiful name, and there the dream ended. A few days later when I happened to be in a nearby city, which is very rare for us, I was walking alone in the crowded street and suddenly saw that everybody was Proverb and that in all of them shone her extraordinary beauty and purity and shyness, even though they did not know who they were and were perhaps ashamed of their names—because they were mocked on account of them. And they did not know their real identity as the Child so dear to God who, from before the beginning, was playing in His sight all days, playing in the world.

In this way Merton came to appreciate himself and his gifts and use them to the full. He came to appreciate God's presence in the world and how much God loved the world and everyone in the world, including himself. His contemplation began to flow into a deep, active concern for all that concerns the human family.

Peter would grow as he walked with Christ in the years that followed. He would come to realize that Christ is indeed the Light of the World, and that the disciple's mission is to bring that light to all the human family. As we reflect on Peter's growth, our own consciousness will expand and will undergo a transformation. We will grow and come to know what it is to be a disciple of the Christ.

The Call to Ministry

As he was walking by the Sea of Galilee Jesus saw two brothers, Simon, who was called Peter, and his brother Andrew; they were making a cast in the lake with their net, for they were fishermen. And he said to them, "Follow me and I will make you fishers of men." And they left their nets at once and followed him.

Going on from there he saw another pair of brothers, James son of Zebedee and his brother John; they were in their boat with their father Zebedee, mending their nets, and he called them. At once, leaving the boat and their father, they followed him. [Matthew 4:18–22]

We do not know how much time elapsed between the first call to Peter and his brother and his friends to become disciples of Christ, and this more particular call that occurred back in their home territory on the banks of the Sea of Galilee. Peter, Andrew, James, and John had returned to their families and their daily labor. But there was a new vision in their lives. They went about their tasks with a new openness to life, to the events of life, to circumstances. They were listening for the Lord in all that they did, all that others said, all that happened. Then one day, as they were busy about their

work, the Master appeared in their midst. He spoke but
a word, and they left their nets at once and followed
him.

We see here how Jesus prepares men, in ways that
perhaps at first they do not perceive, for the mission he
is going to give them. Jesus called these fishermen to
become fishers of men. They could understand his call
because of what had gone before in their lives. And
they would be able to better fulfill their call as fishers of
men because they had spent years as fishermen. They
would have learned many things as fishermen. They
certainly would have learned patience. How often does
the fisherman wait for the schools of fish to come along,
sometimes in vain. They would have learned how to
adapt themselves to those whom they were to serve as
fishers of men. The fisherman has to learn the movements of the fish by patience and discernment, so that
he can use their own movement in order to capture
them for a higher service. It seems destructive of the
fish to capture and kill them so that they might be eaten
by men, yet it is in this way that they are raised to a
higher level of being. The disciples would learn that it
is in dying to our lower selves—which some see only as
destructive—that we are able to come to live a higher
life, a life that is divine. As fishermen, Peter and his
companions learned how to put up with failure and
frustration—how often would they fish all the night
and catch nothing. They would certainly experience
failures as fishers of men. But soon enough, in their
close following of Jesus, they would learn something
else. Often they would do their very best and still fail,
and then suddenly he would turn everything into an

overwhelming success. Then they would clearly see that it was not their skill or labor that brought in the good catch or got them safely to shore, but the grace and care of their Master and their God. As fishermen they learned how to sacrifice themselves, to harden their bodies so that they could give themselves tirelessly to their tasks. They learned how to face storm and danger in order to carry their work forward. These men, who were to carry the message of Christ to every corner of the known world, would need such self-giving stamina.

Oftentimes the particular vocation God has in store for us that will give full meaning to our lives comes only after years of fidelity, a fidelity that can involve an endless number of seemingly everyday humdrum tasks.

The whole world, Christian and non-Christian, is conscious of the tremendous work and mission of Mother Teresa of Calcutta. We are filled with admiration, if not amazement, at her untiring outreach to the poorest of the poor, even those impoverished in the most basic human endowments—unwanted infants and the dying. She brings to each a total love because she transparently sees in each the Lord of her life. But how many are conscious of the fact that Mother Teresa spent many years in the quiet, secluded life of a teaching sister? It was those years of fidelity that prepared her to hear and have the courage to say "yes" to a call from the Lord that led her from the security of her convent to the crowded streets of Calcutta.

Pope John XXIII ascended the throne of Peter at an advanced age—"Here I am, an old man and at the top of the heap"—yet almost immediately he inaugurated a radical transformation of the whole Church. This didn't just happen. This good man spent many years virtually exiled to distant outposts, where he was exquisitely faithful to being before all else a good Christian, a humble servant of God and of his fellow human beings. Witness his deeply moving journal.

We have seen two men emerge from long periods of preparation. John the Baptizer had lived in the desert a very spartan life for some thirty years preparing for his moment. His mission would be brief, but it was the most important prophetic mission in the history of the human race. And like many of the prophets, he would quickly seal his witness with his blood.

Jesus, for his part, except for a brief interlude when he came to official manhood at age twelve, followed the daily life of the ordinary pious Jew. Living in a family, he learned to love, to pray, to work, and to take part in community affairs. He seemed to all to be just the carpenter's son. His was a very ordinary life—a life of preparation. But now his hour has come. He emerges, and the heavens open. The Spirit comes down upon him. God the eternal Father speaks out. And Jesus goes forth on his saving mission.

For most of us, perhaps most of the time, life seems to amble or jog along in a very humdrum fashion. Nothing special seems to be happening. But for each one of us God has a role, a unique and important role, for us to play in the working out of Salvation History. If we are faithful to today's call even in what might seem an uneventful daily life, we will be ready for tomorrow's call, prepared to carry out whatever he might ask of us. "Eye has not seen, nor ear heard, nor has it entered into the heart of the human person what God has prepared for those who love him." Saint Paul quotes Isaiah, and adds: "But the Holy Spirit makes it known to us" (1 Corinthians 2:9–10).

Because Peter had been faithful in seeking to know and do God's will, when the astounding summons came to him, he was ready and able to say yes. We do not know for what God is preparing us. Our mission may always be a hidden and interior one. Who knows how much is accomplished in this fragile and needy world of ours by the quiet, joyful, prayerful lives of those who wait in nursing homes? Unfortunately, more often than we like, we see old folks whose days are filled with bitterness. Instead of blessing God and holding the world in caring love and prayer, they are a bottomless well of laments and complaints. What makes the difference? The years of preparation for this final mission in life.

Jesus is sent forth today in the Spirit by his Father to "open the eyes of the blind, to free captives from prison, and those who live in darkness from the dungeon" (Isaiah 42:7). If we do not see the importance of our everyday life as mission or preparation for the mission the Lord has in store for us, let us ask him this day to open our eyes. If perhaps we already seem a prisoner of meaninglessness or hopelessness, let us ask him to bring us out of the darkness into the light of the vision of hope.

We know that, because we have been baptized in the baptism of the Lord Jesus, the favor of the Father rests on us. We are his beloved in whom he is well pleased. We have but to open our hearts, to let ourselves be washed, so that the Spirit may descend upon us with his love and his peace.

* * *

In this small pericope we can also discern something else. We can see that men of very different temperaments can be and are called to the Lord's service. We see this in the very activities that these men were undertaking when they were called. Peter and Andrew were vigorously at work casting their nets into the lake. James and John were sitting quietly in a boat with their father, mending nets. Peter was that active, vigorous doer whose energies, zeal, and ambition have to be harnessed that they may serve his new mission. John was that more quiet man, subject to authority, who would have to learn detachment and be drawn by the strings of love so that he too could give his all to the service of the Master. In Jesus' service there is a place for those who are by disposition very active and for those who are by disposition more contemplative. Such dispositions may well be signs of the role that we are being called to fulfill in the service of Christ and of his Church. Each one will be led forward to a certain fullness. For one, the contemplative dimension of his life will be filled out and flow into a deepened, active concern for the whole body of Christ, such as we have seen in Thomas Merton. For another, who is more actively disposed, it will be the failures and struggles of his active ministry that will teach him the need to ground himself in a deep contemplative prayer life. By his failures and by the watching and waiting during the endless day between Christ's death and resurrection, and during the long days before the ascension, and in the following years as he sat again and again in prison, Peter learned more and more about the contemplative depths of his own life. John too, with special responsibility in the young Church, learned how to go forth from his contemplative rest on the bosom of Jesus to bring the word of life to far-distant places, to suffer for that word, and even to die in exile.

*   *   *

Another thing that we want to notice here is the fact that Peter is called with others. Back by the Jordan he was with others, his brother and his friends, in his search for a teacher of life. And now, as he is called to apostolic ministry, he is called with them. To be a disciple of Christ is to be called into community. God said at the very beginning of Revelation: "It is not good for man to be alone"—nor woman. The early Christians lived a very communal life, as we see in the Acts of the Apostles:

> These remained faithful to the teaching of the apostles, to the brotherhood, to the breaking of bread and to the prayers. . . .
>
> The faithful all lived together and owned everything in common; they sold their goods and possessions and shared out the proceeds among themselves according to what each one needed.
>
> They went as a body to the Temple every day but met in their houses for the breaking of bread; they shared their food gladly and generously; they praised God and were looked up to by everyone.

Day by day the Lord added to their community those destined to be saved. [Acts 2:42–47]

The whole group of believers was united, heart and soul; no one claimed for his own use anything that he had, as everything they owned was held in common. The apostles continued to testify to the resurrection of the Lord Jesus with great power, and they were all given great respect.

None of their members was ever in want, as all those who owned land or houses would sell them, and bring the money from them, to present it to the apostles; it was then distributed to any members who might be in need. [Acts 4:32–35]

The call to apostolic ministry is usually a call into fellowship with others. The priest is called to be one with the college of priests of the diocese. A man or woman is called into religious community to live and labor together under a leadership that shares the common inspiration of a Founder expressing a particular charismatic aspect of the mission of Christ. Those who are called into a unique mission usually gather others about them to join them in their response to Christ, as we have seen, for example, in the case of Mother Teresa of Calcutta and her Missionaries of Charity.

Because we are weak followers who fall often, it is important that we do have others to help us and encourage us. Think of what it meant to Peter to be able to come together with the other apostles on that first Holy Saturday. On the other hand, it is important that in our own moments of strength we help others. Even if it is a question of a call to live a deeper prayer, we usually need the support of a group to be faithful. It is a commonplace in the charismatic renewal that if we do not regularly attend prayer meetings, soon enough the wonderful graces we have received from the Lord in the outpouring of the Spirit languish and we will no longer make use of them. In teaching Centering Prayer we always encourage people to begin to teach others and to meet with them regularly for prayer so that they will be faithful in their own daily practice and be supported in it.

* * *

Luke places the call of Peter to apostolic ministry in a different context, or perhaps he is just filling out the context that the other two Synoptics have somewhat passed over:

> Now Jesus was standing one day by the Lake of Gennesaret, with the crowd pressing round him listening to the word of God, when he caught sight of two boats close to the bank. The fishermen had gone out of them and were washing their nets. He got into one of the boats—it was Simon's—and asked him to put out a little from the shore. Then he sat down and taught the crowds from the boat. [We know what Jesus taught on this occasion from Mark 4:1–9.]
>
> When he had finished speaking he said to Simon, "Put out into deep water and pay out your nets for a catch." "Master," Simon replied [We see that Simon has already accepted Jesus as his master, has entered into the way of discipleship], "we worked hard all night long and caught nothing, but

if you say so, I will pay out the nets." And when
they had done this they netted such a huge number of fish that their nets began to tear, so they
signalled to their companions in the other boat to
come and help them; when these came, they filled
the two boats to sinking point.

When Simon Peter saw this he fell at the knees
of Jesus saying, "Leave me, Lord; I am a sinful
man." For he and all his companions were completely overcome by the catch they had made; so
also were James and John, sons of Zebedee, who
were Simon's partners. But Jesus said to Simon,
"Do not be afraid; from now on it is men you will
catch." Then, bringing their boats back to land,
they left everything and followed him. [Luke 5:1–
11]

We see here, again, a prefiguring of the future mission
of Simon Peter. It was into Simon's boat, the boat
which Simon commanded, that Jesus stepped and from
which he taught. Later it would be from the bark of the
Church of which Simon Peter was the head that Jesus
would teach the way of salvation across all the seas of
the earth.

We see here something, too, of the human graciousness of Jesus. Peter had put himself at the service of the
Lord. In the end it would be Peter who would reap the
great reward. Our Lord never calls us to serve others,
no matter how self-sacrificing the way may seem, without seeing to it that in the end we are the ones who gain
the most. (Jesus himself came for us and for our salvation, and yet it is he who receives the greatest glory

from his passion, death, and resurrection.) This comes about, though, only if we are open and willing to respond in faith to the Lord. Jesus tells Peter how to find the rich rewards that he wants for him. "Go out into the deep water and lower your nets for a catch." Peter's reason argues that this is not the way. "Master, we have been hard at it all night and caught nothing." The fish are just not running today. Besides, who fishes in the daytime? And yet Peter's openness, Peter's accepting of Jesus as Master, Peter's faith in his Master, enable him to go contrary to his reason, to his instincts as an experienced and successful fisherman: "Master . . . if you say so I will lower the nets." And he caught such a great number of fish that his nets were at the breaking point.

Again we see the importance of community. Peter could not have kept the riches that Jesus had given him if he did not have the support and help of his companions. "They signaled to their mates in the other boat to come and help them. And *together* they filled the two boats until they nearly sank."

One of the things we learn as we go along in the Christ-life is that spiritual gifts and the rich rewards of the Lord, unlike the false rewards of this world, never incline us to pride. Rather, we are humbled and come to realize more and more the immense, complete gratuity of the love of God. One comes to realize more and more one's unworthiness. Peter, seeing how Jesus had so rewarded him for so little, fell to his knees: "Leave me, Lord, I am a sinful man." Even in this statement there is a certain amount of pride. Jesus would take Peter beyond it. Peter speaks as if there was or had to be something in him that merits Jesus' favor. But Jesus' call is completely gratuitous. Jesus would not only give Peter the call, he would give him the grace to accept it gratuitously. One of the great problems we have in the spiritual life is that we constantly want to be able to tell ourselves that we are earning our own way, we are standing on our own feet, we are meriting what we get. But in the end, that can never be the case. This is why Jesus said, "Unless you become as a little child you do not enter into the kingdom." The little child freely accepts all the love, the care, and the gifts which his parents lavish on him. He doesn't have any false illusions about standing on his own feet and earning his own way. We have to humble ourselves and be comfortable with ourselves as children, and accept everything from our heavenly Father as the unmerited gratuity of his overwhelming love. This is indeed humbling. Jesus realized the good will that was in Simon and began to raise him from his fearful, proud self to a truly humble, trusting self. "Do not be afraid." Peter is ready now for the grace of the call to apostolic ministry, the grace that will enable him to leave all and follow Jesus more closely.

Peter's dispossessiveness, at least on the material level, is now complete. It would need more time yet before he would learn to be dispossessed of himself. But the first step has been taken.

* * *

Let me insert a question here. Some time ago the novices gave me a poem entitled "Fish." The first line of it was: "What was Jesus doing while they were pulling in the nets?"

A famous American woman once shared with me the story of her conversion to a living faith. It took place when she was in the House of Representatives. She had just been through a grueling afternoon full of the most tiresome kind of debate. As she reached for her bonnet (it was back in the days when women still wore bonnets), she heard two of the representatives finishing up a conversation. One said to the other, "Well, we can count on the Lord to take care of that." She shot back, "I wish I could say that." The representative was on the ball. He replied, "Go home and read the Gospels the way you would read a bill you are going to vote on in Congress tomorrow, and you will be able to say that." My friend went home, took down the old family Bible and blew the dust off, and began to read Matthew. She read every word, and before the words and after the words and below the words and above the words. She tried not to miss a thing. Before long she was looking for someone to help her understand it all, and was fortunate enough to find an excellent mentor.

As we read these Scripture passages about Peter, we want to savor every word and ask ourselves many questions about what is not being said, what is in between the words. Our Jewish brothers and sisters have the rich tradition of Midrash. Midrash is not a commentary on the words of Scripture in which one explores the various deeper meanings of a word, returning always to the word. Nor is it flights of fantasy. It is rather taking off from a word and finding the fuller meaning that leads on to the next word. It is moving through the Scriptures with the Spirit. The great masters, filled with the Spirit, have shared their experience with their disciples. We each have within us the Greatest of Masters and his Holy Spirit to teach us all things. As we savor the text, we should question the Spirit and allow him to lead us into all truth.

Those of us who cannot encounter Jesus personally in the flesh, as Peter had the great privilege of doing, can encounter Jesus in the Word of Life, in the inspired Word that he has given us in the Sacred Scriptures. For true disciples, such encounters become one of the most important things in our lives. We come with simple and humble faith, something deep within us crying, "Speak, Lord, your servant wants to hear. Lord, reveal yourself. Lord, let me know your love, and then I shall be safe." Scripture study is important. Modern scholarship can at times really help us to break through the barriers of time and culture and language. But there need to be times when we come to the Scriptures in simplicity and faith, relying not so much on our own knowledge and ability to penetrate the meaning as on the Holy Spirit, who inspired the sacred writers and who now dwells in us. We need to come as children to whom belongs the Kingdom of Heaven. We need to come with the same simplicity and openness that marked the humble people of his time who came to hear Jesus on the hillsides and in the synagogues. We need to be aware of the real presence of Jesus in the Scriptures and open ourselves to a true communion with him. We need to seek from him the words that are eternal life.

So what was Jesus doing while they were pulling in the nets? He who said, The Son of Man came not to be served but to serve (Matthew 20:28) certainly wasn't standing there idle. He had the hardened body and calloused hands of a country carpenter. We can be sure he tucked up his robe and bent his back to the work. It would not have been unusual for a rabbi to work, but Jesus did present a picture of a new kind of Master, one who spoke eloquently to Peter. Peter had been the master of this boat, and his ability as a master had been judged by the catches it brought in. Jesus, obviously not an experienced fisherman, going against all the rules of the lake, has taken command and proves himself a consummate master with a literally overwhelming catch.

This not only spoke powerfully to a fisherman about Jesus as Master, but it re-preached the discourse that Peter had just heard as he kept Jesus' floating pulpit stabilized offshore—restated it in the language of the sea. Jesus had used the simile of the soil for his largely agricultural audience:

> Listen! Imagine a sower going out to sow. Now it happened that, as he sowed, some of the seed fell on the edge of the path, and the birds came and ate it up. Some seed fell on rocky ground where it found little soil and sprang up straightaway, because there was no depth of earth; and when the sun came up it was scorched and, not having any roots, it withered away. Some seed fell into thorns, and the thorns grew up and choked it, and it produced no crop. And some seeds fell into rich soil and, growing tall and strong, produced crop; and yielded thirty, sixty, even a hundredfold. . . . Listen, anyone who has ears to hear! [Mark 4:3–9]

Now Jesus, not in word but in living symbol, spoke the same word to the fishermen, and to Peter in particular.

This is why Peter cast himself at Jesus' feet. He knew
he wasn't hundredfold quality. But Jesus knew his man
and what he was to become. Peter himself—yes, he was
sinful and not worthy. But Peter remade, or rather continuing in the creation process that had been going on
since Peter was conceived—"My Father goes on working and so do I" (John 5:17)—that will be something
else. He will not only be worthy, he will be abundantly
fruitful. He will bring in not just a hundred, but a hundred and fifty-three *large* fish (John 21:11). All this lies
for Peter in the future. But for Jesus God, it is all
NOW. For us, discipleship is a patient unfolding, with
the daily discovery of the operation of God's creative
love in our lives until he has fully refashioned us in the
likeness of his Son. This is what discipleship is all
about. It is the recovery of a lost likeness, lost in Adam.
It is the fulfillment of baptism's promise. It is re-creation. It is a coming into oneness that makes us one
with the Son not only in his redemptive mission, where
we are to bear abundant fruit and bring in many fish,
but even in the inner life of the Trinity, where we are
to love and be loved in the unity of the Holy Spirit, who
has become our very own Spirit. This is what the call to
Christian ministry means. A ministry that is not so
grounded in a deep, personal union with Christ in God
cannot be truly fruitful and is not worthy of the name
Christian. It does not flow out of true discipleship.

The Third Call

Jesus now went up into the hills and summoned those he wanted. So they came to him and he appointed twelve; they were to be his companions and to be sent out to preach, with power to cast out devils. And so he appointed the Twelve: Simon to whom he gave the name Peter, James the son of Zebedee and John the brother of James, to whom he gave the name Boanerges or "Sons of Thunder"; then Andrew, Philip, Bartholomew, Matthew, Thomas, James the son of Alphaeus, Thaddaeus, Simon the Zealot and Judas Iscariot, the man who was to betray him. [Mark 3:13–19]

We see three successive calls to Peter. First, the call to discipleship when he accepted Jesus as Master and became his follower, but then went on to live his ordinary life, an ordinary life that would be transformed by a new vision and lead to an ever greater dispossessiveness and openness to the Lord. Then there was the call to apostolic mission, when he had to leave behind the things of ordinary life and follow Jesus more closely and more constantly, and dedicate himself to Jesus' mission. Now we come to the third call, a call to apostolic leadership, to be one of the Twelve.

The first calls were calls to follow Jesus. This third

call is a call to go forth from Jesus with the fullness one
has received in order to bring it to others. The first calls
are calls to the inner life, to building up a personal
relationship with Christ, to a real life of prayer, to a
communion that should develop into a contemplative
union, to the development of the contemplative dimension of life, a deep source of life. Only then is one ready
to receive the apostolic mission to go forth from Christ
but with Christ, always carrying Christ in the depths of
one's being, bringing Christ to others, acting out of the
power of Christ.

It is very understandable that when we first experience the reality of Christ, the meaning he brings to life,
and the immense potential of a heart that is transformed by his grace, we want to go forth and bring this
to others. And we can and should do this, to some
extent. But to pour ourselves out overzealously in ministry and evangelization before we have grounded ourselves deeply in Christ is a great mistake. We have
heard again and again the sad story of burnout, of people who have gone forth with great apostolic zeal into
some of the most difficult missions of the Church, especially that of preaching to the poor that "Blessed are the
poor, for theirs is the kingdom of heaven." And in short
order they have been burned out and have become dis-
illusioned. This happened because they were not
grounded in the Source of power, light, and love, and
their own little share of these resources was very
quickly dissipated. It is very important that those who
are preparing for a life in ministry, whether as priests
or religious, deacons, and lay persons, be given ample
time in the years of their preparation to gain academic

knowledge, pastoral skills, and ministerial experience, but also that they be given ample time to develop a deep personal relationship with Jesus, a deep union with him in love, and a deep centering of themselves in the Source of all life and love, the Divine Presence in the depths of their being. Then when they go forth to ministry they will always be sourced, they will always be able to bring to people the infinite creative love of God pouring forth from the depths of their being. Above all others should those who are called to leadership in the Church be men and women who have come to know by years of intimacy him whom they are to proclaim, him in whose name they are to serve, him who is the Source of all that is life-giving.

Luke notes that Jesus issued this call to apostolic leadership only after he had spent all night in prayer to his Father. "Now it was about this time that he went into the hills to pray and spent the whole night in prayer to God" (6:12). Mark details the special qualities involved in this special call. The Twelve were to be Jesus' companions. They were to be sent out to preach with power. They were to have power "to cure all kinds of diseases and sicknesses" (Matthew 10:1—it is very helpful when we are reading the Gospels to look at parallel accounts to get a fuller picture) and "to cast out devils." Matthew places this call later in his Gospel narrative than does Mark. When Jesus conferred upon the disciples this mission, they had already gone through, as it were, a seminary training. They were taught what to say by listening to Jesus' preaching. Matthew has the proclamation of the basic teaching of Christ, summarized in the long discourse that we call the Sermon on the Mount, precede this mission. They had seen Jesus effect many cures—the healing of the leper, of the centurion's servant, of Peter's mother-in-law—many other miracles, many expulsions of the evil one, and even a resurrection from the dead—Jairus' daughter. Finally, they were given a very explicit instruction on how to comport themselves on their new mission. You can imagine how Peter would have carried out the command to "shake the dust from your feet" of a village that did not accept him! (Matthew 10:14). In Matthew we find a very extensive instruction, far more than the Twelve would need on this first missionary journey. It was meant to be a primer for all future missions. Luke rather contents himself with an instruction for this particular initial mission of the Twelve (Luke 9:1–6).

There have been then three calls for Peter, and we will see later that after his denial of Christ and his return to him, in his restoration Jesus again addresses these three "calls" to Peter.

*   *   *

We are all called. Called first of all in our creation, when we are called from nothingness into life and being for the glory of God. We are called again in our re-creation in baptism—called into an intimate oneness with Christ far beyond anything we can conceive, called to be with him to the glory of the Father in the Holy Spirit. Within these basic calls we are called to partnership, often in the sacrament of marriage, a sign of Christ's union with his Church, or to singleness for the sake of the kingdom. Within these vocations we are called to fulfill other roles among the people of God in the service of the Church or in the service of the whole human family, sometimes successively, sometimes at the same time.

Usually the call does not come in the form of Jesus appearing before us and saying, "Come, I will make you fishers of men." Rather, it comes in the form of interior grace, which enables us not only to perceive the true beauty of a particular mission or way of life, but to perceive it as a good thing for ourselves, a way to live out our life more fully. Then comes the grace that enables us to make a decision to embrace the particular call and to respond to it effectively. Our Lord once said, "You judge a tree by its fruit." The only way that we can be certain about a vocation, a particular call from the Lord, is by the fact that we have been able to respond effectively, for this we can do only by means of his grace. The Lord in his goodness is constantly calling us forth to ever-fuller life. He, in fact, gives us many invitations. He gives us the potential both natural and supernatural to do many things, to fulfill many roles among his people. It is not as though he had some preordained design that we must somehow discover and fulfill if we are ever to find our true vocation. At least, that is not the ordinary case. There are extraordinary vocations. He did personally call the Twelve, and Peter in particular, to fulfill a unique role in his salvific plan. God did send Gabriel to the Virgin Mary, and Bridget to Joan of Arc. He has appeared from time to time to a particular person to give him or her a special call in his Church. But ordinarily it is through the attractions of grace, and the grace to respond to these attractions, that we experience his call, find our vocation, and by the continuing help of that grace come to the fullness of life to which we are ultimately called.

We should not make a great mystery out of vocational discernment. Nor a tortuous process. With and after serious prayer, we should give ourselves a reasonable amount of time to explore our different possibilities and seek adequate counsel. If at the end of such a serious search the matter is not yet clear, we can take it that Jesus is saying to us, You choose what you want to do for me. We must then have the courage to use the freedom he has given us and choose a particular path, fully determined to live it to the full, and generously abandon the alternatives for its sake—something that is not always easy to do. Then we need to say to the Lord, You have left the choice to me. I choose this. I know you have the power to make it the very best, and in your love for me, you are going to make it the very best —for you, for me, for all.

In the end, it is only love that matters. The call is to a way of love, to grow in love. Our "yes," like Peter's, is a commitment to love.

Mother-in-Law

On leaving the synagogue, Jesus went with
James and John straight to the house of Simon and
Andrew. Now Simon's mother-in-law had gone to
bed with fever and they told him about her
straightaway. He went to her, took her by the hand
and helped her up. And the fever left her and she
began to wait on them. [Mark 1:29–31]

Jesus was becoming well known as a rabbi, a teacher
with his own disciples and followers who traveled about
with him. Yet he had no intention, nor was there any
need, of establishing a sect apart. When he came to
cities and towns he went to the regular synagogue ser-
vices. He remained always a part of institutional religion, he took part in the liturgical prayer of the community. So did his disciples and followers, until the
community of the faithful had developed its own insti-
tutions and liturgical prayer. Institutional structures
and liturgical prayer are in no wise inimical to true discipleship of Jesus. If we follow his example and that of
his first disciples, we will be fully part of the institutional Church and will take part in the life of the
Church with its liturgical prayer as faithfully as we can.

On this particular occasion, since they were in Peter's hometown, after the service in the synagogue they

went to Peter's house. Peter, whom the Church honors
as the first Pope, was a married man. We have spoken
about vocation and call and have seen how there can be
vocations within a vocation. Many Christian commu-
nions freely accept married persons for priestly and apostolic mission. In the United States and other coun-
tries the Roman Catholic Church has begun to ordain
married men who were married and in ministry before
their reception into the Church. There can also be second vocations—a call to the ministry of the priesthood
after a full married life. Perhaps this was the case with
Peter. He had completed his vocation as a husband and
father—if ever he were a father—and was now responding to another call from the Lord.

This chapter would be better written by a married
man who would know something about a man's relationship with his mother-in-law, what that can mean in
his life and in his response to Christ. The only mother-
in-law I have ever known intimately was my own
mother. She had three daughters-in-law, and I saw how
different was her relationship with each of these
daughters. I wonder in what ways Peter's relations with
his mother-in-law changed when he became a disciple
of Christ.

Usually most of our relations come out of what I call
"reaction." When we first come into this world we are
extremely dependent. We develop our first external relationships with the basic material necessities of life:
our need for nourishment, for warmth, and for strok-
ing. As our consciousness expands, we become aware of
the people who provide these needs for us. As we develop somewhat further, we become aware of the

things we can do, and significant persons usually rein-
force our sense of value through our doing. "That's
mother's good little boy," when we put away our blocks.
"Mommie won't love you if you don't eat your carrots."
We come to define ourselves by what we have, by what
others think of us, by our doings insofar as they are
evaluated by others. We create a false self, a self made
up of our responses to things and persons extrinsic to
ourselves. These come to determine how we think and
act. This is what I mean when I speak of relating out of
reaction. Eventually God comes into the picture as the
Great One we have to please in order to gain the ultimate things we need: eternal life and the fulfillment of
our deepest desires. The false self created by extrinsic
evaluation tends to be a very fragile self. It has to be
defended and protected at all times. Hence we become
very defensive, protective, and competitive; we seek to
aggrandize ourselves by putting others down.

What we need in order to attain the dispossessiveness of the disciple of Christ is a real transformation of
consciousness. Rather than beholding God as distant
from us, the ultimate rewarder of whatever good we
manage to accomplish, we need to see him at the center
of our being, as our very source. We need to realize that
his act of creation is not something done once and for
all. At every moment, we are coming forth from the
fullness of his creative love.

Remember that scene in the Gospel: One day a rich
young man ran up to Jesus and said, "Master, what
must I do to gain eternal life?" Jesus answered him and
said, "Why do you call me good? One is good, God." He

was inviting the young man to witness that Jesus is God. But he was also affirming a basic reality: One is good, God. All goodness, all being, all life comes from God. It is not exactly accurate to say that God made us and everything else out of nothing. Rather, he shares with us something of his own being, beauty, and life. Everything that is, is and is good and beautiful because it shares in God's being, goodness, and beauty. If we see things truly, we see this to be the case. If we truly know ourselves, we know that at the depths of our being is an infinitely loving, creative God who ever more and more brings us forth into being, sharing with us something of his own being, goodness, and beauty. In this love we see our true selves as we are in God and coming forth from him. We know how affirmed and loved we are by him. Coming from this Source, no longer do we have to defend a fragile false self. Rather, coming from our true self, we become a creative source of life for ourselves and for everyone else. We create the relationships that support life. Peter as a disciple would come to know his true self in the love he received from Christ, his Friend and his Master, but also his God and his Creator. And out of that love he would create a beautiful relationship with his mother-in-law. It was because of that beautiful relationship, because of the deep, caring, loving way Peter held his mother-in-law in his heart, that Jesus, when he entered Peter's home, immediately stretched out his hand in healing to the afflicted woman. When we are in touch with our true selves and the power of the love that is within us, we create the kind of relations we want. And because these relations are flowing out of the Source of Creative Love, they are a source of healing and wholeness.

Shortly before, in response to the faith of the centurion of Capernaum who had generously endowed the synagogue, Jesus had exclaimed, "I tell you solemnly, nowhere in Israel have I found faith like this" (Matthew 8:6). Jesus saw in the heart of Peter something greater than faith; he saw concern, love, and care. And to these he could not but respond.

One of the first things we learn from this particular incident in the life of Peter is something about prayer of intercession. We notice that Peter does not ask Jesus to cure his mother-in-law. He had just witnessed the marvelous power of Jesus in the synagogue, where the Lord not only freed a man from a long-standing bondage to an evil spirit, but it seems even raised him to life when the spirit had left him as though he were dead. Peter makes no petition, but Jesus immediately responds. Responds to what? What Jesus responds to, what he hears, is not the words of our lips but the *concerns of our hearts*. We don't have to try to remember to pray verbally for all the different people who have asked us to pray for them, for all the different cares and concerns that have been brought to us or have risen in our own lives. We don't have to rattle off a long litany of needs. If you ask me to pray for you, the important thing is not that I remember you next time I go to prayer, and it will probably do you little good if I just rattle off a couple of "Our Fathers" for you. The important thing is that I place you in my heart and hold you with concern and love so that when I next do go to

prayer, Jesus will see you there and will extend his healing and blessing hand.

I think this is brought out in the Gospels not only in
this instance, but in a couple of other very important
instances involving two great women of prayer, Mary
the Mother of Jesus, who ever pondered in her heart,
and Mary of Bethany, who chose the better part and sat
at Jesus' feet. For one, Jesus worked his first miracle,
and for the other, his greatest miracle, before and
prefiguring the ultimate miracle of his own resurrection. If the two Marys do express aloud their concern, it
is so that we can be in on the happenings. "They have
no wine" (John 2:3). At Cana we can see Jesus even
squirm a bit. After all, how will it sound going down in
sacred history that the first sign the Son of Man worked
on earth was turning out more booze for the boys after
they had drunk the house dry? Undoubtedly the fact
that he had arrived at the party with his band of newly
gathered disciples had something to do with the embar-
rassing shortage. He could not deny the concern of the
heart of the one he loved most in all the world. Nor
could he deny the other Mary. "The man you love is ill"
(John 11:3). He tarried to give them yet a greater gift
and sign. And he mingled his tears with hers, sharing
her grief, before he renewed the life of her brother.

These Marys did not ask anything from the Lord. It
was to their concern that Jesus responded. Peter, in
bringing Jesus into his life and into his home, brought
him into all his concerns. And Jesus immediately responded to them in his caring, loving, gratuitous cure of
Peter's mother-in-law.

Peter had witnessed Cana; it was the first sign he

had seen Jesus work. It made a powerful impression on him. He undoubtedly had it in mind when he brought Jesus to his own home that Sabbath morning. He may not have thought precisely of the healing of his mother-in-law, but he knew that in bringing Jesus into his home, it would be blessed in some special way. The home of every disciple should be a place where Jesus is welcomed. The enthronement of the Sacred Heart used to be a popular Catholic practice. Some formal reception of the Lord into a new home and some visible sign of his presence, such as a shrine, statue, or icon, can prove a very real blessing to the disciple. Most disciples will have their hidden sanctuaries of prayer where they go in quietly and close the door and pray to their Father in secret (Matthew 6:6). It is well, though, also to have a shrine where the household can gather for prayer on a regular basis as well as in times of special need or thanksgiving—a shrine that proclaims to all who enter that this Master has been welcomed into this house as the Master of the house because he is the Master of those who dwell therein.

* * *

The healing power of Jesus was now released. Immediately there followed a whole spate of healing, as Mark tells us: "That evening, after sunset, they brought to him all who were sick and those who were possessed by devils. The whole town came crowding round the door, and he cured many who were suffering from diseases of one kind or another; he also cast out many devils, but he would not allow them to speak, because they knew who he was" (Mark 1:32–34).

Another scene in the Gospels indicates how much such a healing ministry cost Jesus. One day, as he was pushing through a dense, jostling crowd, a poor afflicted woman who had suffered many years dared to reach out with faith to touch the hem of his garment. Faith is always rewarded; she was immediately healed. Power went forth from the Lord. Jesus turned around and searched the crowd with his eyes and let it be known that he felt the power going forth from him (Luke 8:43–46). If the Master cannot minister healing comfort without power going forth from him, how much more is this true of the disciple? We find Jesus early the next morning, before anyone else was up, going off into the hills to pray. There he would commune with his Father in the Spirit of Love that bound them in oneness, and touch the Source of the power of his ministry.

If we hope to exercise a powerful, healing ministry, we need to go forth regularly from the crowd, from the insistent demands of ministry, even if it means forgoing sleep and rising early. We need to be alone with our Master, in communion with his Father and ours, in the Love who is the Holy Spirit. We need to return to the Source, know the presence and power within us, and know the bountiful freedom that is ours when we minister out of this Source.

* * *

"In the morning, long before dawn, he got up and left the house, and went off to a lonely place and prayed there. Simon and his companions set out in search of him, and when they found him they said, 'Everybody is looking for you.' He answered, 'Let us go elsewhere, to the neighboring country towns, so that I can preach there too, because that is why I came.' And he went all through Galilee, preaching in their synagogues and casting out devils" (Mark 1:35–39).

We can imagine Peter's reaction when he woke up and found that the Master was gone. There were many reasons for his alarm and concern. He certainly sensed his call to follow Jesus closely, to be a special disciple of the Lord. An affection was growing up between them. Peter was coming to love this man and did not want to be parted from him. There was also another side, I am sure. Peter was delighted the night before when the whole town gathered at *his* door and he was seen to be the great benefactor of the village, for he had brought the Master and all his healing power. Peter did not want Jesus to go away. He quickly roused the other disciples, and they went in search of Jesus. They already knew him well enough to know what he was up to and where he would be found. Soon enough they came upon him secluded among the knolls of the nearby hills, praying to his Father. Peter blurted out his concern: "Everybody is looking for you." Jesus knew and understood the false pride and ambition that still lurked in Peter's heart. He would in no wise nurture it. They would not to go back to Peter's house and make that the center of his apostolic ministry. "Foxes have holes and the birds of the air have nests, but the Son of Man has nowhere to lay his head" (Matthew 8:20). They would go forth to the other towns of Galilee. They would go to the lost sheep of the tribe of Israel. They would bring his healing and his love and his word

of life to anyone who would listen. Peter, whose discipleship of Jesus was becoming more important to him
than his self-serving love, would humbly follow his
Master. He still had a lot to learn.

Putting His Best Foot Forward—Into His Mouth

Called though he was to discipleship, to apostolic ministry, and even to leadership, Peter was still Peter. He was still prone to speak all too quickly. He would be a long time in learning. Fortunately, he had a Master of infinite patience.

The day of the first miraculous multiplication of loaves and fishes gives us a good example of Peter's impetuosity. It had been quite a day! It had begun with the sad news that John the Baptizer, the one to whom Peter and his brother Andrew and their friends had first turned in the hope of finding a word of life, had been beheaded (Matthew 14:13). John was Jesus' cousin. But John meant much more than that to Jesus. The news of his death was shockingly painful. Jesus' immediate reaction was to invite his disciples to go apart with him "to a lonely place where they could be by themselves." But by this time Jesus was too much the man of the hour. The people always had their eyes on him, and news of his movements quickly spread. Jesus' hope to find a "lonely place where they could be by themselves" was quickly frustrated. When he put ashore with his disciples, "a large crowd was waiting" to receive words of life, and healing for their sick. The compassionate heart of Jesus could not but respond. The day was consumed with teaching and healing. Night was soon approaching. The disciples, no doubt with the practical Peter at their head, came to the Lord: "This is a lonely place, and the time has slipped by; so send the people away, and they can go to the villages to buy themselves some food." Jesus' response caught them off guard: "There is no need for them to go; Give them something to eat yourselves." They had already looked to see what they had for themselves. "All we have with us is five loaves and two fish." "Bring them here to me," Jesus said (Matthew 14:15–18).

Jesus proved himself quite practical, and soon had the disciples busily sitting the people down in orderly groups—he knew somebody would want to take a count before the evening was over. Then Peter and his fellow disciples had the astonishing experience of receiving a few bits of bread and fish from the Lord and handing them out, and handing them out, and handing them out, and still having bits of bread and fish. Their growing amazement! They remembered the widow's pot of oil (2 Kings 4:1–7) and the jar of meal at Zarephath (1 Kings 17:7–16). There was indeed a great prophet here, and more than a prophet.

In his busyness and excitement, Peter hardly had time to reflect and realize that five loaves and two fish, when they are our five loaves and two fish, are only five loaves and two fish. But when they are received as a gift from the hands of the Lord—Jesus "took the five loaves and two fish, raised his eyes to heaven and said the blessing. And breaking the loaves he handed them to his disciples"—they are the resources to accomplish anything and everything the Lord wants us to do.

If the disciples had insisted on keeping the five loaves and two fish for themselves, there would not have been enough for a decent meal for them. And they could well have expected friends and neighbors and others, too, to press in on them for a share. Indeed, fights might have soon broken out as each one grabbed for his bit—as in our world today. When our mentality is one of scarcity and selfishness, the end result is scarcity, and oftentimes jealousy, resentment, and fighting. But when the disciples in faith generously turned over what they had to the Lord for the use of all his people, then not only did everyone have enough, but in the end they came away with "twelve full baskets." The generosity of the Lord in response to any generosity we show is pressed down and flowing over.

Yes, it had been quite a day. The banquet was over. All were satisfied—at least in regard to their physical hunger. Other desires could now surface—confused desires, unfortunately, for no one yet understood the Master. Jesus sent his disciples on their way lest they get into trouble, and then he slipped away into the mountains, as was his custom, to replenish his forces in quiet prayer and communion with the Father. He would catch up with the Twelve a little later.

As the Apostles made their way across the lake in their boat, they experienced the difficulty of being without the Lord. They had to battle with a heavy sea and contend with a strong head wind. Things were always easier when he was present. After a long night of struggle, in the last part of the night, the Lord did come.

How often it is that the Lord leaves us to struggle as if we have to make it on our own before he comes to our aid! If he comes too soon, we are all too prone to credit ourselves for what he does. It is only when we have a deep experience of our own limitations and helplessness that we can begin to appreciate how truly it is that only by his grace do we accomplish all we accomplish.

Some years ago I was counseling a couple of fine young men who were eager to enter the monastery. Both of these lads were struggling with the problem of masturbation. And they were really struggling with it. One day, being quite angry with the Lord, I demanded of him why he did not help these men overcome their weakness so that they would be free to follow him in the way they wanted. The next morning, as I was sitting in the spiritual father's room in our guesthouse, a man who had been coming to our monastery for many years knocked on the door. He too had had a long, hard struggle—his was with alcohol. Recently he had struck rock bottom and now, by a great gift of God's grace, he had found his way into Alcoholics Anonymous. With the enthusiasm of a new convert, he began to tell me about this wonderful program. It wasn't my first experience with AA, and I knew what was coming. I sat back, ready to hear the twelve steps. But as he began to recount the first step—a man must admit to himself, to God, and to some other person that he is a hopeless case—a bell rang for me. I realized then what was going on with the two young men I was counseling. What the Lord had taught this man through alcohol, and was teaching others through an angry temper, or a proneness to gambling, or a constant struggle with distractions in prayer, the Lord was teaching my young men through their struggle with masturbation. It is only when we have done our utmost, have struggled with all the energy in us and still have failed, that it finally comes home to us in our guts that we cannot do it ourselves, and that all the good that is accomplished in us is accomplished by God's grace. Once we realize this, God can do anything he wants in our lives because there is no longer any danger that we will take the credit to ourselves. God loves us with an immense love and he has given us everything, even his own Son. But there is one thing that God cannot give us and still be God, and that one thing is his glory. We are so prone to put our own initials at the bottom of the work. But as long as we claim anything as coming ultimately from ourselves, God is no longer God. We have made a false God—ourselves. So the Lord often leaves us struggling through what seems like a long night of the spirit so that we can learn what it is to be without him, what the results are when we try to accomplish things solely by means of our own resources. It is only when we have really learned how limited we are that he then comes in the "fourth watch of the night" and brings us deliverance.

He made the disciples get into the boat and go on ahead to the other side while he would send the crowds away. After sending the crowds away he went up into the hills by himself to pray. When evening came, he was there alone, while the boat, by now far out on the lake, was battling with a heavy sea, for there was a head-wind. In the fourth watch of the night he went towards them, walking on the lake, and when the disciples saw him walking on the lake they were terrified. "It is a ghost," they said, and cried out in fear. But at once Jesus called out to them, saying, "Courage! It is I! Do not be afraid." It was Peter who answered. "Lord," he said, "if it is you, tell me to come to you across the water." "Come," said Jesus. Then Peter got out of the boat and started walking towards Jesus across the water, but as soon as he felt the force of the wind, he took fright and began to sink. "Lord! Save me!" he cried. Jesus put out his hand at once and held him. "Man of little faith," he said, "why did you doubt?" And as they got into the boat the wind dropped. The men in the boat bowed down before him and said, "Truly, you are the Son of God." [Matthew 14:22–33]

Peter, the commander of the fleet, was still the dauntless seaman. The long struggle of the night had not taught him anything. In fact, he was still buoyed up by the experience of the day before when he saw in his own hands bits of fish and bread multiplied to feed thousands. Jesus' "Don't be afraid" only challenged him. In his enthusiasm he cried out, "Lord, if it is you, tell me to come to you across the water."

Jesus loved Peter, and he knew what was in him. He wanted to encourage this enthusiastic faith. He also knew that Peter had lessons to learn. Without hesitation Jesus replied, "Come."

I wonder if Peter experienced any hesitation once he heard the "Come." The ship was tossing around wildly

in a rough sea. Was he so buoyed up, so enthusiastic
that he stepped over the side without another thought
and went bounding across the water toward Jesus? I
suspect so. If he had hesitated for a moment I think his
faith would have quickly floundered. For soon enough,
"as soon as he felt the force of the wind, he took fright
and he began to sink." First his faith began to sink, then
he followed right after it. And yet there was that spark
of faith. He knew his Master. He still had confidence in
him. "Lord! Save me!" And "Jesus put out his hand at
once and held him." They walked back to the boat hand
in hand. Held securely by the Lord, Peter's love over-
came all doubt, all fear.

And those in the boat? They watched the whole
wondrous spectacle. They were perhaps not surprised
by Peter's outlandish request. They knew him well
enough. But they were stupefied when they saw him
actually jump out of the boat and run across the water.
When he began to sink, that made sense. When Jesus
reached out and the two of them walked peacefully and
safely toward the boat, a mixture of emotions washed
through their minds and hearts. As the Master stepped
in they fell down on their knees in awed adoration:
"Truly you are the Son of God." Lucky for Peter they
were so awed, or he might well have heard some gibes
about a fisherman not making a very good fish or a
"Rock" that quite naturally sank.

The fact remains: Peter did walk on the water, and
he walked on it *with Jesus*. From the moment that Jesus
reached out and grasped his hand, Peter knew that
Jesus would take care of him. Later he would advise us:

"Cast your care upon him for he has care of you" (1 Peter 5:7).

The next day, when the people again crowded around Jesus, the Master challenged them in regard to the bread and sought to raise their thoughts and desires to that Bread of which yesterday's was but a prefiguring. The Eucharist is our constantly recurring multiplication of loaves. But for many, Jesus' banquet of love was too much. Such a communion was "intolerable." "Many of his disciples left him and stopped going with him."

Then, with a heavy heart, Jesus turned to the Twelve: "What about you, do you want to go away too?" Peter, in the power of the faith that he had drawn from the saving hand of Christ, dared to respond in the name of all: "Lord, to whom shall we go? You have the words of eternal life, and we believe—we know that you are the Holy One of God" (John 6:67–69). Job had asked: "Where does wisdom come from? Where is understanding to be found?" (Job 28:12). Peter now knew: "You have the words of eternal life."

This is a fundamental perception for a disciple. The Master has wisdom and is a source of wisdom. He is able and willing to impart it to those who would become his disciples. The disciple of Jesus knows that Jesus is the Source of all Wisdom. He is Wisdom itself. He is the Way, the Truth, and the Life.

This was one of Peter's better moments. How full his life was of ups and downs—his days on the waves and the luck of the fisherman were perhaps meant to prepare him for this.

"The Holy One of God," his very Son—how quickly

Peter would let this realization slip into the back of his mind.

* * *

Peter did not always get off so easily when his mouth got ahead of what his mind should have told him.

> When they reached Capernaum, the collectors of the half-shekel came to Peter and said, "Does your master not pay the half-shekel?" "Oh yes," he replied, and he went into the house. Before he could speak, Jesus said, "Simon, what is your opinion? From whom do the kings of the earth take toll or tribute? From their sons or from foreigners?" And when he replied, "From foreigners," Jesus said, "Well then, the sons are exempt. However, so as not to offend these people, go to the lake, cast a hook: take the first fish that bites, open its mouth and there you will find a shekel; take it and give it to them for me and for you." [Matthew 17:24–27]

For me this is one of the more humorous incidents in the life of Peter. At the same time, it has a very touching element.

Here is Peter, as usual, too ready to speak up. Often enough Jesus has been challenged with his disciples or because of his disciples by the upholders of the Law. So when they come and challenge Peter: "Does your Master not pay the half-shekel?" Peter is all too quick to say, "Yes, yes, he pays." Poor Peter, he doesn't even have a chance to defend himself. When he comes in, immediately Jesus challenges him and calls upon Peter to convict himself. "Peter, now who does pay the tax? The

Son or the servant?" Peter's own logic won't let him escape. Then Jesus, without rebuking Peter, with a great deal of understanding, and with powerful pedagogy, sends Peter off to get the tax money. Here he is, the great fisherman, the commander of a Galilean fleet, sent off with a little line and a hook to stand by the seashore to wait for some particular little fish to nibble on his hook. We can be sure the other disciples didn't lose the opportunity to enjoy Peter's discomfiture. As he stood there doing the only thing he could do, trying to wait patiently, he could hear the taunting voices: "Peter, has the fish bit yet?" "Come now, great fisherman, where's this fish?" "Oh Peter, you really are a sight!" Perhaps he did not have to struggle with his rising temper as much as he ordinarily might, diverted as he was by his own reflections on his stupidity and his proneness to put his foot in his mouth.

Finally the little fish did nibble on his hook, and up it came. A very relieved Peter found, as he pulled the hook out of the fish's mouth, that there was also a shekel to be drawn out. The touching part of this story is the fact that Jesus tells Peter to find not just a half-shekel for Jesus' tax, but a whole shekel for his own *and* Peter's tax. There is no other place in the Gospel accounts where Jesus so personally and immediately identifies himself with a human being: "for me and for you." This bit of human delicacy undoubtedly did much to salve the discomfiture that Peter experienced as he sought to learn again and more deeply not to be so quick to speak up out of his own presumptuous spirit, especially when he was taking the responsibility to speak for his Master.

When we disciples speak out to set forth the teaching and the claims of our Master, we must be very sure that what we say is indeed faithful to who he is and to his claims upon us.

* * *

On another occasion Jesus' response to Peter's presumptuousness was not quite so humorous. It seems as though his patience was wearing a bit thin.

> From that time Jesus began to make it clear to his disciples that he was destined to go to Jerusalem and suffer grievously at the hands of the elders and chief priests and scribes, to be put to death and to be raised up on the third day. Then, taking him aside, Peter started to remonstrate with him. "Heaven preserve you, Lord," he said, "this must not happen to you." But he turned and said to Peter, "Get behind me, Satan! You are an obstacle in my path, because the way you think is not God's way but man's." [Matthew 16:21–23]

Jesus had just acknowledged the work of the Father in Peter preparing him for the important mission as the rock on which Jesus would build his Church. Taking heart from Peter's clear confession, Jesus went on to begin to prepare Peter and the others for the dark hour that lay ahead when they would have to see their Master "suffer grievously at the hands of the elders and chief priests and scribes and be put to death." Peter was feeling his oats, having just been praised highly by the Lord. He wasn't ready for the scandal of the cross. So he took Jesus aside and started to remonstrate with him: "Heaven preserve you, Lord," he said. "This must not happen to you." Jesus didn't mince words as he put a pin directly into Peter's balloon. "Get behind me, Satan. You are an obstacle in my path, because the way you think is not God's way but man's."

I think we all at times enjoy the fantasy: Well, if I had been God I would have arranged things in this world a little better. It takes us a long time to absorb fully those words of Isaiah: "My thoughts are not your thoughts, nor my ways your ways, but as high as heaven is above the earth, so are my thoughts beyond your thoughts and my ways beyond your ways." God's ways will not be our ways often enough, and we have to be humble enough to listen, to wait, and to learn. In a word, we have to be true disciples as the Lord patiently teaches us and draws us up toward his level of consciousness so that we can understand, or at least accept in faith and hope, the mystery of the cross. It is only through death that we come to the new life of the risen Christ.

Jesus didn't waste any time in beginning to impart this to his disciples. He immediately went on to say to them, "If anyone wants to be a follower of mine, let him renounce himself and take up his cross and follow me. For anyone who wants to save his life will lose it; but anyone who loses his life for my sake will find it" (Matthew 16:24–25).

* * *

Peter's quickness to speak up was not always to his embarrassment. His blunt questions often provided the occasion for Jesus to teach us basically important things.

Peter was willing to display his mystification at the parables of Jesus—"Explain the parable for us" (Matthew 15:15)—and get for us, who are usually equally mystified, the explanations we need. His question, "Lord, how often must I forgive my brother who wrongs me? As often as seven times?" opened the space for Jesus to proclaim the new dispensation of mercy and love: "Not seven, I tell you, but seventy times seven" (Matthew 18:21–22)—that is, without ceasing. Jesus went on to tell the parable of the unforgiving debtor: "And that is how my heavenly Father will deal with you unless you each forgive from the heart" (Matthew 18:35).

And then there was that far from disinterested question: "What about us? We have left everything and followed you. What are we to have then?" (Matthew 19:27). Surprisingly, this didn't evoke from Jesus a remonstrance, a call to unselfish love. There would surely be many occasions when he would call for that. Well might he have pointed out to Peter that he hadn't left all that much: a few boats, probably leaky, nets that always needed to be mended, and lots of hard work. Rather, Jesus made, not only to Peter but to all of his followers, an offer that is hard to refuse: "Everyone who has left houses, brothers, sisters, father, mother, children or land for the sake of my name will be paid a hundred times over and also will inherit eternal life"—a mighty good investment.

I have a little joke going with the Lord. When I was preparing to enter the monastery, my brother, who was at that time not too keen about my monastic vocation, offered me the opportunity to go to Europe to spend as

much time as I wanted doing whatever I wanted before
entering. When I spoke to the vocation father about
this, he saw it as a tactic to try to divert me from responding directly and immediately to the Lord, and he
advised me not to accept this opportunity, but to give it
up for the Lord. Contrary to all expectations, in the
years that followed, again and again my superiors directed me to Europe, first for studies and then for various activities of the Order. And I keep saying to the
Lord, "Really, Lord, I don't want a hundred trips to
Europe!"

After responding directly to Peter, Jesus went on to
teach the parable of the vineyard laborers (Matthew
20:1–16). It doesn't matter really how much the disciple leaves behind. It doesn't matter whether he was a
laborer from the first hour, or the third, or the sixth, or
the ninth, or the eleventh. The thing that matters is
that when we hear the call we respond and leave everything for Christ's sake, to give ourselves completely to
the Lord.

It was Peter who pointed out "the fig tree withered
to its roots"—"Look, Rabbi, the fig tree you cursed has
withered away"—and afforded Jesus the opportunity to
give to Peter, a man whose weakness in faith he had to
chide, and to all of us, a lesson on the power of faith.
"Have faith in God. I tell you solemnly, if anyone says
to this mountain, 'Get up and throw yourself into the
sea,' with no hesitation in his heart but believing that
what he says will happen, it will be done for him." And
the call to pray with faith: "I tell you therefore: everything you ask and pray for, believe that you have it
already, and it will be yours" (Mark 11:20–24).

When Jesus spoke of the forthcoming destruction of the great Temple of Jerusalem, it was Peter's question, "Tell us, when is this going to happen, and what sign will there be that all of this is about to be fulfilled?" that afforded Jesus the opportunity to speak at length not only of the coming destruction of Jerusalem, but even of the end times and the signs and distress that would precede them (Mark 13:1–8).

A certain ingenuous simplicity before the Lord certainly has its value. Even if it does lead at times to embarrassment, it can be the occasion, with its openness, to receive from the Lord the important teaching that we need. Unfortunately, all too often we are for putting on some sort of pretense. We want people to think we are wiser than we are, that we understand when we don't, that we have the answers. And in doing this we block the possibility of our Master teaching us what only he can teach. We fail to seek from him the words of true life.

We do not want to imitate Peter's impetuosity, but we do want to risk his complete childlike openness and trust, for "anyone who does not welcome the kingdom of God like a little child will never enter it" (Mark 10:15). Only those who want to learn and can trust can become in any true sense disciples of the Master.

Prayer

Six days later, Jesus took with him Peter and James and his brother John and led them up a high mountain where they could be alone. There in their presence he was transfigured: his face shone like the sun and his clothes became as white as the light. Suddenly Moses and Elijah appeared to them; they were talking with him. Then Peter spoke to Jesus. "Lord," he said, "it is wonderful for us to be here; if you wish, I will make three tents here, one for you, one for Moses and one for Elijah." He was still speaking when suddenly a bright cloud covered them with shadow, and from the cloud there came a voice which said, "This is my Son, the Beloved; he enjoys my favor. Listen to him." When they heard this, the disciples fell on their faces, overcome with fear. But Jesus came up and touched them. "Stand up," he said, "do not be afraid." And when they raised their eyes they saw no one but only Jesus. [Matthew 17:1–8]

Tabor remains one of the most beautiful spots in all the land that Jesus and Peter knew so well through constant traversing. Perhaps one reason why I found Tabor so beautiful is that it is the only spot sacred to the memory of Jesus that is safe from the onslaught of hoards of tourists—it is too steep for the tourist buses to climb. It remains a place of sanctuary, a summit of transfiguring beauty.

It was not long after Peter's confession of the Messiahship of Jesus at Caesarea Philippi and Jesus' confirmation that Peter was gifted by the Father with a deeper understanding of who Jesus is that the Lord led Peter, James, and John up this high mountain. I think in this pericope we have a very important teaching on prayer.

First of all, in order to enter into prayer, it is necessary to follow Jesus with faith and confidence, and to go with him to a place where we can be alone with him. Peter and his companions did not know where Jesus was leading them. The way was rugged. But they followed with faith and with confidence. Finally they came to a summit. And *there* Jesus was transfigured.

It was a moment that engraved itself deeply in Peter's memory. Years later, as an old man, he would write to the Churches and remind them, "We had seen his majesty for ourselves. He was honored and glorified by God the Father, when the Sublime Glory itself spoke to him and said, 'This is my Son, the Beloved; he enjoys my favor.' We heard this ourselves, spoken from heaven, when we were with him on the holy mountain" (2 Peter 1:16–18).

The sacred writers struggle for images to bring out the radiance of the transfigured Christ. Matthew says that his face shone like the sun and his clothes became white as light (Matthew 17:2). Mark says his clothes became dazzling white, whiter than any earthly bleacher could make them (Mark 9:3). And Luke says his clothing became brilliant as lightning (Luke 9:29). It was an awesome spectacle. But it was to be made even more awesome. For then there appeared with Jesus the holy Prophet Elijah and the great lawgiver of the people, Moses. And they spoke with Jesus.

For the Jews, revelation was usually summed up in the expression "the Law and the Prophets." Moses was the one who gave them the Law. Elijah was one of the greatest of the prophets, the one who was brought beyond the lightning and beyond the roaring of the storm to the still, small voice that revealed the inner life of God. Both these men had a special experience of God on the holy mountain of the Jews, Horeb or Sinai. And now they appear on this mountain with Jesus. The Old is fulfilled. That to which it pointed, toward which it ever moved, is at hand. What this tells us is that it is through the sacred writers, through the Sacred Scriptures, and through the whole of Salvation History, that we are to come to know our Lord and understand his mission and its meaning for our lives. It is through listening to the Word that we will be led into deep, transcending prayer where the Presence and the love of the Triune God will be revealed to us.

Mark, who is considered to be Peter's scribe, says of Peter that "he did not know what to say" (Mark 9:6). But Peter was never one to be at a loss for words. He knew that he was filled with an immense joy and himself transfigured in this awesome moment of Presence. He wanted it to continue. And so he babbled out something about building three tents. He probably had in mind the sort of tents or fragile little buildings of reeds that the Jews built at the Feast of Tabernacles to remind them of their time of passage through the wilderness.

Luke was probably on the mark when he said that Peter did not know what he was saying (Luke 9:33). As he spoke, the theophany became even more awesome. A luminous cloud, perhaps not unlike the one that descended on Sinai, now came upon this holy mountain and overshadowed them. The disciples found themselves within the cloud. Then the Father spoke. This was too much for Peter and the others. They fell on their faces. No longer could Peter even babble, he was so overcome with fear. The classical Byzantine icon shows the three disciples strewn in different directions, with their sandals flying this way and that. The Lord sometimes has to clobber us pretty hard before we learn that prayer is not a monologue but a dialogue, and it behooves us, as the disciples, to stop babbling and listen. This was the Father's message to the ebullient Peter and his companions: "This is my Son, the Beloved; he enjoys my favor. *Listen to him.*"

Luke tells us that Peter and his companions "were heavy with sleep, but they kept awake" (Luke 9:32). He has a similar report at Gethsemane, but there they didn't keep awake. The Evangelist-Physician sees this as an effect of fear. Sleep is one of the ways in which we try to escape our fears and other negative emotions. In the Garden of Gethsemane Peter did give in to sleep and escaped from his fear and grief rather than staying with his Lord in anguish and prayer. But here on Tabor that was not the case. Here we have some effort to describe the state of contemplative prayer. One of the greatest teachers of prayer that the Christian tradition has ever known, Saint Teresa of Avila, says that when one first enters into a more contemplative type of prayer, one has many misgivings, one wonders if anything is happening, if one is not just falling asleep. Since we are used to passing from the waking state to the sleeping state, when we first begin to pass from the waking state to the contemplative state the only thing we can call up from our past experience is the passage into sleep. It seems similar to us until we become more familiar with the contemplative state, and the great difference between it and sleeping. As the Scriptures say, "I sleep but my heart watches." On Tabor, indeed, Peter's heart watched and there was given to him a great revelation, the first inklings of the fullness of the Trinitarian mystery. The Father spoke to him and gave him a powerful word of life: "This is my Son, the Beloved; he enjoys my favor. *Listen to him.*" This of course is the first and most fundamental principle of all discipleship: to listen to the Master.

When the theophany was over, Jesus himself leaned down and touched Peter with the hand that had become so familiar to him. The tenderness called him forth from his fear. "Stand up. Do not be afraid." Matthew reports that "when they raised their eyes they saw no one but only Jesus." This is a result of contemplative prayer. There develops in us a real connatural sensitivity that becomes aware of God in everybody and everything, that becomes sensitive to the presence of Christ in each of his beloved, that comes to know the whole Christ as a living reality and begins to respond to everybody and everything according to the truth of their being in God.

* * *

As they came down from the mountain, Jesus gave Peter and his companions a very difficult order and one that might have seemed to them very curious. They were to tell no one about the theophany until the Son of Man had risen from the dead. This "risen from the dead" seems to have gone completely over their heads. Instead of asking about it, they asked about Elijah. In his response Jesus again gave them a warning of what lay ahead. He told them that in John the promise of the Prophet's coming before the Messiah had been fulfilled. And then, pointing to the way they had treated John, he told them that the Son of Man would suffer similarly.

Peter and his companions had been drawn into a very special relationship with Jesus. Jesus' teaching had been opened to them more profoundly than to the people at large. They had seen day after day the power of Jesus going forth, not only overcoming all the weaknesses and ills of human persons, but also conquering the powers of the evil one, of the demonic kingdom. They were ready for a more sublime revelation. And they needed it to strengthen them for the trials that lay ahead, of which Jesus was beginning to warn them. The people as a whole were not yet ready for the full manifestation of Jesus' divinity, and even less so for the awesome mystery of the Trinity.

The true disciple of Jesus, especially the disciple who is called to the ministry, has to learn how to move at God's pace and not at the pace that might be dictated by his own wisdom or enthusiasm. He must respect the way God's grace is working in him and in others, and move in harmony with it. To get ahead of it can only hurt, frustrate, and even destroy the action of that grace in life.

Peter had grown enough now not to be dominated by the very human drive for self-importance. He might have been tempted to vaunt the particular knowledge he had received on the mountain, to pride himself on the special grace that was given to him in the revelation of the transfiguration. But no word of this splendid mystery passed from his mouth until the Son of Man was risen from the dead. In fact, as we see Peter struggle with his own fidelity to Christ in the midst of the Passion, we wonder if the memory of it was obliterated from his own mind and heart. It certainly was there later, as we have seen. It may have been overclouded. So often, in the time of temptation, the light that shone so brightly when we were at prayer seems to be gone. All is obscure. When the time came for an open witness to the Lord Jesus in the fullness of his divinity, Peter would be able with humble pride to recall that he was with the Lord on the holy mountain.

* * *

We grow both by depth and by expansion. On Tabor Peter was led into the very depths of God in the revelation of the Trinity. He would spend the rest of this life, and eternity itself, plumbing the full significance of what he first caught a glimpse of on the mountain. It was another prayer experience that expanded his conscience and enabled him to see more the length and breadth of the significance of the creative presence of

God in the universal call of the Incarnation of God in the humanity of Christ:

Peter went to the housetop at about the sixth hour to pray. He felt hungry and was looking forward to his meal, but before it was ready he fell into a trance and saw heaven thrown open and something like a big sheet being let down to earth by its four corners; it contained every possible sort of animal and bird, walking, crawling or flying ones. A voice then said to him, "Now, Peter, kill and eat!" But Peter answered, "Certainly not, Lord; I have never yet eaten anything profane or unclean." Again, a second time, the voice spoke to him, "What God has made clean, you have no right to call profane." This was repeated three times, and then suddenly the container was drawn up to heaven again.

Peter was still worrying over the meaning of the vision he had seen, when the men sent by Cornelius arrived. They had asked where Simon's house was and they were now standing at the door, calling out to know if the Simon known as Peter was lodging there. Peter's mind was still on the vision and the Spirit had to tell him, "Some men have come to see you. Hurry down, and do not hesitate about going back with them; it was I who told them to come." Peter went down and said to them, "I am the man you are looking for; why have you come?" They said, "The centurion Cornelius, who is an upright and God-fearing man, highly regarded by the entire Jewish people, was directed by a holy angel to send for you and bring you to his house and to listen to what you have to say." So Peter asked them in and gave them lodging.

Next day, he was ready to go off with them, accompanied by some of the brothers from Jaffa. They reached Caesarea the following day, and Cornelius was waiting for them. He had asked his relations and close friends to be there, and as Peter reached the house Cornelius went out to meet him, knelt at his feet and prostrated himself. But Peter helped him up. "Stand up," he said, "I am only a man after all!" Talking together they went in to meet the people assembled there, and Peter said to them, "You know it is forbidden for Jews to mix with people of another race and visit them, but God has made it clear to me that I must not call anyone profane or unclean. That is why I made no objection to coming when I was sent for . . ."

Then Peter addressed them: "The truth I have now come to realize," he said, "is that God does not have favorites, but that anybody of any nationality who fears God and does what is right is acceptable to him.

"It is true, God sent his word to the people of Israel, and it was to them that the good news of peace was brought by Jesus Christ—but Jesus Christ is Lord of all men. . . ."

While Peter was still speaking the Holy Spirit came down on all the listeners. Jewish believers who had accompanied Peter were all astonished that the gift of the Holy Spirit should be poured out on the pagans too, since they could hear them speaking strange languages and proclaiming the greatness of God. Peter himself then said, "Could anyone refuse the water of baptism to these people, now they have received the Holy Spirit just as much as we have?" [Acts 10:9–47]

Peter went to the housetop about the sixth hour to pray, still observing the regular prayer times of the pious Jew. In fact, for Peter and the other disciples they were becoming the prayer times of the new Christian community. To this day, at least in monasteries, the third, the sixth, and the ninth hour are times when the members of the community leave off their work and come together for prayer.

Peter was still fully human. The sixth hour is near midday, and naturally enough, "Peter felt hungry and was looking forward to his meal." In the few minutes before that meal was served—for minutes of time can be great spaces in the realm of the Spirit and eternity— Peter was to have a mind- and heart-expanding experience. The very heavens were to open to him and he would be brought into the experience of the heavenly Father on the sixth day, when God looked upon his creation and realized that it was good.

Under the old dispensation, the Father took care of a primitive people on pilgrimage by making many basic hygienic laws sacred, as they should be, for we are sacred—the whole of our being and everything that concerns us are the concern of God. But God's loving dispositions for yesterday are not always those for today, nor today's, for tomorrow. We must be ready to move with the Lord of History as he speaks to us through the signs of the times and through his Body, the Church. The practical hygiene that God had raised to the level of the sacramental had unfortunately become too much of the essence of religion for God's chosen people. Like ourselves, they were prone to latch on to the externals, which we humans can manage, in order to avoid the deeper things, which we cannot manage but which rather manage us and lead us into the realms of contemplation, transcendence, and adoration. Peter was to lead the new Christian community into the freedom of the children of God; he himself had to be free. If the salvation that was first of all to the Jews was to be to all peoples, then Peter had to know that all peoples are dear to God. And so in this hour, when Peter was open to God in prayer, he was taught the great lesson that "what God has made clean you have no right to call profane."

We see Peter led step by step by the Spirit according to the needs of the Church. The Spirit had to tell him, "Some men have come to see you. Hurry down and do not hesitate about going back with them. It was I who told them to come." Peter, like all of us, was too inclined to get caught up with what he had just learned. He wanted to stay with this astounding new experience of God. But God wants us always to move on, to share what we have learned from him and bring it into the life of the community. What we receive from God is never just for ourselves; it is for the whole Church, the whole of the People of God. One way or another, we are called upon to share it. Peter went down and said to them, "I am the man you are looking for. . . ." He was ready to go with them.

Peter was not slow to learn: "The truth I have now come to realize is that God does not have favorites, but that anybody of any nationality who fears God and does what is right is acceptable to him." This is a profound truth that we all need to learn and realize fully. If we search deeply in our hearts, I am afraid most of us are apt to find we do harbor there some prejudices, some subtle attitudes in regard to the relative merits or worth or performance of one or another particular race or nationality. We all tend to have our "Samaritans," and see the good found among them as something exceptional. For Jesus and his true disciples, there are only sons and daughters of God—his brothers and sisters, and ours.

How often has the mission of the Church to bring the word of salvation been undermined and even blocked by a certain pride on the part of the messengers, of those called to the apostolic ministry. When I was in India I had lunch in a convent of nuns who had been missionaries in India for many decades and prided themselves on the good work they were doing. There was no doubt much could and should rightly be credited to them. We sat at a long table with a number of Irish sisters, and below them a number of Indian sisters. The Irish sisters thought they had recently made a great breakthrough in acculturation in allowing the Indian sisters to put off the heavy European habits the Irish sisters wore in favor of the *kavi,* the orange-colored sari, that was the native religious garb of India. I had on my way to this convent visited a number of ashrams and so did not find this change at all surprising. It was a step in the right direction. But I was struck by the fact—and mentioned it—that this was the first time I had ever seen Indian women eating with knives and forks and spoons and that it seemed very strange to me. The Indian sisters clapped their hands with joy. They were happy that I appreciated their native culture and their right to preserve it. The Irish sisters were not so happy about my remarks. They thought that they had brought one of the benefits of "civilization" to the Indian sisters in teaching them to eat with these utensils, instead of respecting the sisters' culture and allowing them to eat as their people have always eaten. This is just a very small example. It can be multiplied many times and in many more important areas. The expression given to the theology of the Church has until recently universally required all peoples, in order to embrace Christian teaching, to become Aristotelian or Platonic thinkers of the Greco-Roman tradition. The Second Vatican Council has opened the way to let native peoples receive the simple biblical revelation and express it according to the philosophical concepts that belong to their own culture. The worship of many Christian peoples has also been marred by the almost universal requirement to follow the Roman liturgy. Now we are beginning to allow peoples to take the treasures of their own culture and use them in the worship of the true God just as the first Greek and Roman converts did.

Having seen the great difficulty that some Church leaders in our times have experienced in moving with the breadth of the Spirit in the Church of the Second

Vatican Council calling for radical renewal, we are all the more in astonished admiration of Peter. As he readily admits here, he was brought up in a rather strict and narrow mentality that had taught him from the earliest days of his life not to associate with people of other religions and cultures. "You know it is forbidden Jews to mix with peoples of another race and visit them, but God has made it clear to me that I must not call anyone profane or unclean." Peter was ready to learn, ready to let go of his past, ready to move on. And thus he was worthily chosen to be the first leader of the Christian Church, for its call was to be open to all nations, to all peoples, to all cultures, and to all traditions. The Jewish believers who were with Peter were not quite so ready to move, and it took a powerful outpouring of the Holy Spirit with his charismatic gifts to make them realize the new breadth of the Spirit of God among the peoples of the nations. Peter for his part was not slow to proclaim, "They have received the Holy Spirit just as much as we have." When he returned to the apostles and brothers in Jerusalem, he did his best to help them understand what he had learned. He shared openly and humbly the gift he had received from the Lord, even though he knew that many would not receive it and would think less of him for it. But as he spoke honestly and openly, his account "satisfied them and they gave glory to God" (Acts 11:18).

One of the most important fruits of prayer is that it should open us to hear God and allow his grace to bring about in us a transformation of consciousness. If we are stuck with prayer forms, if we are trying to satisfy ourselves and prove our own righteousness in our prayers, if we are too busy saying formulas to stop and create spaces of silence and openness to hear God, then something is radically wrong with our prayer. Prayer is a conversation. In any good conversation we must not only speak, but also listen. We need to develop a habit of listening in prayer, especially since in this conversation the one to whom we address ourselves is the source of all wisdom. How presumptuous it is for us to do all the talking and expect him to do all the listening! But it is not enough just to listen. We must listen with a readiness to respond, even if it means giving up value systems, prejudices, and lifelong traditions and practices. We must humbly realize that no matter how old and wise might be the thoughts and ideas and traditions by which we live, for the wisdom of God they are the nonsense of children. "My thoughts are not your thoughts, nor your ways my ways, says the Lord, but as high as heaven is above the earth so are my thoughts beyond your thoughts and my ways beyond your ways." We must come to prayer seeking to hear God and be led into his ways and his thoughts, and be empowered by the Spirit. Then can we open the way for the outpouring of God's love, grace, and peace in the Holy Spirit. Then can we give effective witness to our fellows that will enable them to step forward into a new consciousness of the ways of an all-merciful and all-loving God.

The Peter who here exclaims, "Certainly not, Lord; I have never eaten anything profane or unclean" is the same Peter who cried, "You will never wash my feet!" But in another sense, it is not the same Peter. The same impetuosity might well be there, but it comes from a humbled and enlightened heart that knows it has yet much to learn. In docility to the Lord, Peter will be led where he does not want to go, but where the Lord wants him to go and where he will be an instrument of the Spirit of life and love.

We see, then, in this brief account of a day in the life of Peter, first of all, the importance of regular times of prayer and fidelity to them. What would have happened if on this particular day Peter had decided to skip the sixth hour of prayer that he usually practiced, if he had not been there to see the heavens open and receive the message of the Lord? We never know what we miss when we omit one of our regular periods of prayer or meditation. We see here, too, something of the expected effects of prayer. True prayer expands our consciousness so that we begin to see things God's way and not just our way or the way of the institution, the tradition, or the laws. Peter's first answer has the savor of the Pharisee about it. "Never have I eaten . . ." He is led to go beyond the law, beyond the security of fulfilling the law, to walk in the way of obedience to God in the Spirit. There is an expansion in his outlook as he sees the whole of creation under a different light. There is an expansion in his activity as he goes forth to be one with Gentiles. And there is expansion in his power as his very words open the space for a great outpouring of the Spirit.

Through fidelity to prayer, and to a prayer that listens, we will learn to hear God and grow with God and be the effective instruments in his hands that he and we want us to be. We will most probably not be favored with any such extraordinary external vision as that reported here, even if we are most faithful to our times of prayer. But as we enter into deep prayer, we will come to know by a certain experience that at every moment we are coming forth from the creative love of God. And not only ourselves, but the whole of creation. And we will know the intrinsic goodness of every human person made in the image of our God. And like our Master, we will want to reach out in compassionate and redeeming love. We will be true disciples.

A Saving Glance

From time to time some of the monks of my monastery visit a nearby Orthodox monastery. It is always refreshing and challenging to come into contact with this fervent expression of our own Christian monastic tradition. As is his wont, the Spiritual Father of the monastery usually presents us with an icon. On the occasion of one of our visits he gave me a very unusual icon. It is simply the head of Christ, but it is Christ in that moment when "he turned and looked straight at Peter" (Luke 22:61), after the cock had crowed announcing Peter's third denial of Jesus. I hung the icon in my cell. I must confess that I have often been tempted to remove it, for each time I look upon it, it is like a stab in the heart. The Lord is now looking at me, and he reminds me how like Peter I am. I think and act as though I were strong, but in fact I am very weak; I let what others think decide my course of action. But the icon reminds me too—which is why I keep it—that no matter how abysmal my failure may be, if like Peter I can have the humility to weep for my sin and stay with the community, I can, by the grace of the Lord's own Resurrection, rise to new strength and courage in his service.

I believe that in that moment when Jesus looked at

him, we have a key moment in the life of Peter. Before that moment, he was Simon. "Simon, Simon! Satan, you must know, has got his wish to sift you all like wheat; but I have prayed for you, Simon, that your faith may not fail, and once you have recovered, you in your turn must strengthen your brothers" (Luke 22:31–32). He had been a weak man with whom Satan would all too frequently have his way. But after the saving glance, he was Peter: "You are Peter and on this rock I will build my Church and the gates of the underworld can never hold out against it" (Matthew 16:18). The power of the glance of Christ.

This is perhaps the key element of true prayer, that kind of prayer in which we are truly convicted by the Lord, brought to true conversion, and empowered by the grace of the Resurrection. Saint Paul would later write, "For those who love God all things work together unto good." And another great saint would add, ". . . even sin" (Saint Augustine). When Jesus was seized in the garden, all the disciples deserted him, fleeing through the underbrush and trees seeking to save their own skins. But Peter had the courage to come out of the bush and at least "follow at a distance." He failed, he failed miserably, but at least he was there to receive the healing, saving glance of Christ. When we go to prayer, all too often we try to avoid that glance. We keep busy with our own thoughts, our own ideas, our many words, our liturgical formulas. We avert our glance so that we do not have to see him, we do not have to meet him eye to eye. But there is power in the glance of Christ.

Right up to this ultimate moment of conversion we

see the same bravado in Peter. Jesus had sent him with John to prepare the Supper. As we noted before, they are in a way representatives of the two classic types: the contemplative and the activist. They were together in their call. They were sent together by Christ to prepare this meal that he "longed with a great longing to eat with them," to bring to completion his new covenant, the Sacrament of his Body and Blood (Luke 22:18). They would be together with Jesus in the Garden and following him after he was seized. They would be together running to the tomb. At the Last Supper they sat one on Jesus' right and the other on his left.

There is more than one way to follow Jesus. No one is excluded from discipleship. Each can follow according to that temperament and grace which the Lord has given him. No one temperament is of itself better than any other. Each is of the Lord.

Jesus knew that the Father had put everything into his hands, and that he had come from God and was returning to God, and he got up from table, removed his outer garment and, taking a towel, wrapped it around his waist; he then poured water into a basin and began to wash the disciples' feet and to wipe them with the towel he was wearing.

He came to Simon Peter, who said to him, "Lord, are you going to wash my feet?" Jesus answered, "At the moment you do not know what I am doing, but later you will understand." "Never!" said Peter. "You shall never wash my feet." Jesus replied, "If I do not wash you, you can have noth-

ing in common with me." "Then, Lord," said Simon Peter, "not only my feet, but my hands and
my head as well!" [John 13:3–9]

There is one thing very refreshing about Peter's bravado: he doesn't get stuck in it. He is very ready to
move and become just as enthusiastic in the opposite
direction. This freedom came from his overriding devo-
tion to his Master. His basic enthusiasm was to be a
true disciple. As soon as he saw what that called for, he
was completely there. Peter was, in some very real way,
to stand in the place of Christ in the midst of the infant
Church after his Master had ascended into heaven. He
had to learn the way of true leadership within the
Christian community, the way of service. He learned it.
Deep in his gut he experienced swirls of emotional tur-
moil as he sat there and watched his Master wash his
feet, fulfilling the office of a slave in his regard. It would
be an unforgettable lesson. Jesus' disciples had all too
often argued among themselves as to who was greatest,
and vied for the first places in the Kingdom. They
would never do that again. They heard deep in their
own beings that he who would be first must take the
last place.

But all the bravado had not yet been extinguished in
Peter. As Jesus went on to speak sorrowfully of the
things that were to come, Peter was again presump-
tuously making claims: "Although all lose faith in you, I
will never lose faith. Even if I have to die with you, I
will never disown you." And Jesus had to respond with
that most dire of predictions: "I tell you most solemnly,
before the cock crows you will disown me three times."

The words cut deep, very deep. Never again do we hear a presumptuous word from the mouth of Peter. And yet the words themselves were not enough. A lived experience of his own terrible, self-betraying weakness was needed to bring him finally to that self-knowledge that would enable him to grow with a dispossessive humility to all the greatness to which God was calling him.

We all know the sad story.

First there would be the failures in the Garden. Leaving the rest, Jesus took Peter and the two sons of Zebedee with him into a more solitary spot. An immense sadness came over him, and great distress. He said to them, "My soul is sorrowful to the point of death. Wait here and keep awake with me." And going on a little further, he prayed. "My Father," he said, "if it be possible, let this cup pass from me. But nevertheless let it be as you, not I, would have it." He came back to the disciples and found them sleeping. And he said to Peter, "And so you had not the strength to keep awake with me one hour. You should be awake and praying not to be put to the test. The spirit is willing but the flesh is weak" (Matthew 26:36–41). We know this sad scene was repeated a second time, and a third. This "Rock," who said he would even go to prison and to death with Christ, could not stay awake one hour with him in his anguish. Luke adds a very telling remark. He tells us that "Jesus found them sleeping for sheer grief." Sleep is one of the means we use to avoid life, its demands, its anguish, its potentials.

Then we come to the second betrayal: "Judas the traitor knew the place well, since Jesus had often met his disciples there, and he brought the cohort to this place . . . Simon Peter, who carried a sword, drew it and wounded the high priest's servant, cutting off his right ear. The servant's name was Malchus. Jesus said to Peter, 'Put your sword back in its scabbard; am I not to drink the cup that the Father has given me?' " (John 18:2–11). And Luke adds: "Touching the man's ear, Jesus healed him" (Luke 22:51).

Again Peter was playing the role of Satan, trying to stand between Christ and the fulfillment of the role that the Father had given him. An all-too-human love of his Master held him back from embracing who his Master truly was, from being completely one in union and communion with his Master in embracing the Divine Will. In striking out, he did violence to all that Jesus stood for: to healing, to reconciliation, to nonviolence. As Jesus reached out and healed Malchus' ear, he took another step in his all-healing mission.

And Peter headed for the bush.

But the disciple's love was strong, and it brought him out of the bush to follow, at least at a distance. His love was strong—but not strong enough to keep him from the final fall, the final betrayal.

Peter was sitting outside in the courtyard and a servant-girl came up to him and said, "You too were with Jesus the Galilean." But he denied it in front of them all. "I do not know what you are talking about," he said. When he went out to the gateway another servant-girl saw him and said to the people there, "This man was with Jesus the Nazarene." And again, with an oath, he denied it, "I do not know the man." A little later the bystand-

ers came up and said to Peter, "You are one of
them for sure! Why, your accent gives you away."
Then he started calling down curses on himself
and swearing, "I do not know the man." At that
moment the cock crew, and Peter remembered
what Jesus had said, "Before the cock crows you
will disown me three times." And he went outside
and wept bitterly. [Matthew 26:69–75]

It is Luke who adds, "The cock crew and the Lord
turned and looked straight at Peter" (Luke 22:60–61).
Throughout Luke's account we find a certain tenderness toward Peter. Remember, he was the one who
used Mary as his source. It is Luke who tells us that at
the very time that Jesus was foretelling Peter's denial,
he told him, "I have prayed for you, Simon, that your
faith may not fail, and once you have recovered, you in
your turn must strengthen your brothers" (Luke 22:32).
It is Luke who notes that after one of the disciples (he
doesn't mention Peter by name) struck the high priest's
servant and cut off his right ear, Jesus "touching the
man's ear, healed him," giving us hope that when in our
misguided zeal we hurt others, Jesus in his loving mercy
will bring the needed healing. And finally, in the account of the denials he leaves out everything about Peter's cursing and swearing; rather, he has him say simply, "I am not him, my friend."

Is denial a part of discipleship?

Sad to say, for us poor, weak, sinful humans, it is.
Inevitably we do fail Jesus, our chosen Master. What is
revealing here in Peter, and consoling for us because it
is so true in our own lives, is the fact that we fail in the

little challenges. Peter had said to Jesus, "Even if I have to die with you, I will never disown you." (And note that all the other disciples said the same.) If in the Garden the soldiers had successfully grabbed hold of Peter and led him off with Jesus, Peter probably would have been loyal all the way to the cross—as he one day would be. But now we see that the gibe of a little serving-girl makes him cower and betray himself, his loyalty, his love, and his Master.

Yes, all we disciples will fail. But then what are we to do?

Peter gives us the example. The moment he realized his failure, the moment Jesus looked at him, "he went outside and wept bitterly." We are to repent. But repentance is not enough. Judas repented, too. He returned his ill-gotten gain to the Temple. But then he went out and hanged himself. Peter, on the other hand, returned to the community. A profoundly humbling experience. Can you imagine his feelings the first time he walked into the midst of the other disciples? He who was to be the leader, he who had made such proud boasts at the Last Supper—and now they all knew it, they knew that three times he had denied his Master. He denied even knowing Jesus, not to speak of being his disciple.

The temptation is very great, when finally we are confronted with our weakness and our failures, to give up. If we do not, like Judas, go so far as to hang ourselves from a tree, we are tempted at least to withdraw from the community, to withdraw from the apostolic ministry, to withdraw from being an engaged disciple of Jesus. How many priests and religious—I have heard the story so often—have entered into apostolic ministry with tremendous zeal, but soon are caught up, more unconsciously than consciously, in a driving activity motivated increasingly by human respect, by the need to be wanted and to be affirmed, by ambitions and temporal goals. More and more they neglect the time they need to continue to deepen their relation with the Lord and to be sourced and strengthened by him. "You should be awake praying, not to be put to the test. The spirit is willing, but the flesh is weak." Sometimes they go on for as much as a decade or more before burning themselves out. Then one day they realize that the very reason they answered the call and entered into the apostolic ministry and the fullness of discipleship has been completely neglected and lost sight of. They are filled with regrets and repentance. But instead of turning back to the community and seeking its help, strength, and guidance to be renewed in the deeper meaning and vision of their call, they throw in the towel and seek another way. Peter returned to the community and so he was ready, he was in place to receive the summons to reconciliation with the Lord.

Mark, who gives us Peter's catechesis to the early Church, makes much of the fidelity of the women to Jesus. They stayed with him to the very end: "There were some women watching from a distance. Among them were Mary of Magdala, Mary who was the mother of James the younger and Joset, and Salome. These used to follow him and look after him when he was in Galilee. . . . Mary of Magdala and Mary the mother of Joset were watching and they took note of where he was laid" (Mark 15:40–47). The great Peter was scared away by a little serving-woman, but these good women stood fast right to the end. Rightly then was it a woman to whom the Risen Lord first announced his victory over death, a woman he sent to the great Peter to challenge him again to break through his fears into faith. Mary Magdalen "came running to Simon Peter and the other disciple, the one Jesus loved. 'They have taken the Lord out of the tomb,' she said, 'and we don't know where they have put him' " (John 20:2). The man who had received the saving glance was no longer afraid to be known as a disciple of Jesus, to make a fool of himself.

So Peter set out with the other disciple to go to the tomb. They ran together, but the other disciple, running faster than Peter, reached the tomb first; he bent down and saw the linen cloths lying on the ground, but did not go in. Simon Peter who was following now came up, went right into the tomb, saw the linen cloths on the ground and also the cloths that had been over his head; this was not with the linen cloths but rolled up in a place by itself. Then the other disciple who reached the tomb first also went in; he saw and he believed. Till this moment they had failed to understand the teaching of scripture, that he must rise from the dead. [John 20:3–9]

Mark tells us that it was an angel who directed Mary Magdalen: "You must go and tell his disciples and Peter" (Mark 16:7).

"Yes, it is true. The Lord has risen and appeared to Simon" (Luke 24:34). That first encounter between the

Risen Lord and the repentant disciple who had betrayed him three times is so sacred, so intimate, so special that we are only told that it happened. The details are fully hidden in the hearts of two lovers, a Master and his disciple. The public reconciliation and reinstatement of Peter will come later.

At the root of any true Christian ministry, if it is to be true and effective, must be a personal relationship with Jesus; otherwise the ministry is a charade. First Peter's personal relation with Jesus had to be healed and the healing take full possession of him before he could unhesitatingly affirm it publicly, even three times, and be ready to stand as Christ's vicar, the good shepherd of his flock, the head of his Church.

The Other Side of the Man: The Rock

When Jesus came to the region of Caesarea Philippi, he put this question to his disciples, "Who do people say the Son of Man is?" And they said, "Some say he is John the Baptist, some Elijah, and others Jeremiah or one of the prophets." "But you," he said, "who do you say I am?" Then Simon Peter spoke up, "You are the Christ," he said, "the Son of the living God." Jesus replied, "Simon son of Jonah, you are a happy man! Because it was not flesh and blood that revealed this to you but my Father in heaven. So I now say to you: You are Peter and on this rock I will build my Church. And the gates of the underworld can never hold out against it. I will give you the keys of the kingdom of heaven: whatever you bind on earth shall be considered bound in heaven; whatever you loose on earth shall be considered loosed in heaven." Then he gave the disciples strict orders not to tell anyone that he was the Christ. [Matthew 16:13–20]

Luke, who so often brings special nuances to these occasions, tells us that "when he [Jesus] was praying alone in the presence of his disciples he put this question to them" (Luke 9:18). As we search the Scriptures we find that before every significant event Jesus takes time for prayer. He sought more and more to draw his disciples into this practice. Before his ultimate test there would be a heartbreaking attempt as Peter and the others slumbered in Gethsemane. But they did learn. We find them spending days in earnest prayer awaiting the coming of the Holy Spirit in the epiphany of the Church at Pentecost.

We come now to one of the climactic moments in the mission of Jesus and the consummation of Peter's call to discipleship. Jesus is a good teacher. So he first seeks to clear the space, removing the superficial influences: "Who do people say the Son of Man is?" We are all influenced, perhaps much more than we realize, by what other people say and think. It is only by some conscious reflection on where our opinions or thoughts or prejudices are coming from that we can begin to realize that they are not truly our own. Then we can lay them aside in order to look more deeply into our hearts and see what are truly our own personal convictions, the sources of our life's conduct.

After clearing away other peoples' conjectures, Jesus then put his finger on his own disciples, and specifically on Peter, whom all by this time would expect to be the spokesman. "But you, who do you say that I am?" Peter comes up with the right answer: "The Christ, the Anointed One of God, the Son of God, the Messiah." It is difficult for us who have not lived in and been formed by an intensely religious Jewish culture to grasp the significance of this affirmation, all the connotations that

that word, the Christ—the Messiah—held for a pious Jew—the burden of centuries of history, of election, of exodus, of promise, of covenant. Certainly Peter did not understand the full weight of what he had said, especially when he added, "the Son of the Living God." This is why Jesus went on "and gave the disciples strict orders not to tell anyone that he was the Christ." There were too many false ideas and false expectations with regard to the Messiah. This is very evident from the next scene, when Jesus begins to bring out for the Twelve the fact that the Messiah, the Christ, the Anointed One, is also the Suffering Servant of Isaiah. Peter for one was not ready for this. He was scandalized by it. He was not ready to embrace the mystery of the cross. And so our Lord did not want him or the others to attempt to speak yet about his true identity.

Much harm is done within the Christian community because those who are proclaiming the Word really do not know what they are talking about. If they really did, they could not live the way they do. Like Peter, most Christians have the words but do not understand what they truly mean. We "know" that God is love, but we do not know what this means when it comes to living as a disciple of Christ. Cardinal Newman in his writings makes the distinction between a "notional assent" and a "real assent." We have the notions. We accept them. Christianity for us too often is just that: acceptance of certain notions and ideas. What we need is that "real assent," that profound understanding that calls forth the response of our whole being. As Chesterton has said, "Christianity has not failed. The problem is that it has never been really tried." To live love—that is what

Christ did. That is what we his disciples must do to be true disciples. Not parrot formulas. And above all, not try to force our formulas, no matter how right and sacred, down the throats of others. Or persecute others because they won't parrot them with us. Rather, like Christ our Master, we disciples need to lay down our lives with all their certainties and formulas, to embrace our brothers and sisters, and to serve them with self-giving love. But such a life-giving truth cannot come from ourselves.

Jesus told Peter, "It was not flesh and blood that revealed this to you, but my Father in heaven." The revelation of the divinity of Jesus Christ, and his sonship, and his unity with the Father in the Holy Spirit who is Love is not a notion that can come from anywhere except God himself. It is a revelation of the inner life of God. Even the notions, and being able to say "yes" to them, are an immense grace. At the Last Supper Jesus promised that the Holy Spirit, the Paraclete, would come and would teach us all things: "The Advocate, the Holy Spirit, whom the Father will send in my name, will teach you everything and remind you of all I have said to you" (John 14:26).

At baptism we received what have been called the theological virtues, the virtues of faith, hope, and love, by which we are able to believe what God has revealed to us and place our hope in him and love him in a way that is worthy of him. But also in that moment when we were made partakers of the divine nature, there were implanted within us certain dispositions by which we can operate beyond the human mode, even the human mode strengthened with the theological virtues of faith and hope. These dispositions have been called the gifts of the Holy Spirit. These dispose us to allow the Spirit to guide us according to the divine instinct, far beyond what our human mind, even with the help of the virtues, can attain. This is the purpose of a deeper, more contemplative type of prayer. We leave off the thoughts and reflections and ponderings of the rational mind and open the space for the Spirit to operate within us. Through the gifts he will give us a deep experiential sense of who God is and who we are in God and what it means to be disciples of a Master who is Love. It is only when we can let go of our more superficial selves and enter into a prayer of profound listening that we can come to that living and life-giving knowledge of Jesus Christ that will enable us powerfully and effectively to proclaim that he is the Christ, the Son of the Living God, and live in accord with what we are proclaiming. Peter as a disciple had begun to learn to listen. We, as disciples, need to begin to make space in our lives for divine learning by a daily practice of listening prayer. The simple method of Centering Prayer is a good way to begin this.

"You are Peter and on this rock I will build my Church." This proclamation of Peter's special office corresponded to a role that was natural enough to this forceful man from the shores of Gennesaret, and was indeed already being exercised. Peter had a natural gift for leadership, and the other disciples willy-nilly respected it. Grace was building on nature. From whom did the nature come?

Jesus would speak of Peter's special role in relation to his fellow disciples again at the Last Supper, even as he warned of Peter's weakness and failures: "Simon, Simon! Satan, you must know, has got his wish to sift you all like wheat; but I have prayed for you, Simon, that your faith may not fail, and once you have recovered, you in your turn must strengthen your brothers" (Luke 22:31–32). His special role was recognized in the announcement of the Resurrection. The angels told the women, "You must go and tell his disciples and Peter" (Mark 16:7). "And running to the tomb," John showed deference to Peter, for he did not enter, although he arrived first, until Peter had entered in. After the ascension of Jesus into heaven, it was Peter who led the community of disciples in choosing a successor for Judas (Acts 1:15). He became the spokesman for the disciples from Pentecost onwards. His leadership was confirmed with awesome power in the case of Ananias and Sapphira (Acts 5:3), and also in healing—even his very shadow healed people (Acts 5:15). Saint Paul acknowledged the particular preeminence of Peter after his conversion: "I went up to Jerusalem to visit Cephas and stayed with him for fifteen days, I did not see any of the other apostles" (Galatians 1:18–19). Even though he "opposed Peter to his face," he always acknowledged Peter's special call.

I do not want to develop here a theological treatise on the primacy of Peter. What I want to bring out is that there are reasons why the power to bind and loose that Jesus confers here is usually considered to be a special prerogative of Peter and his successors. On Easter Sunday Jesus will stand in the midst of his disciples and he will breathe on them and say, "Receive the Holy Spirit. For those whose sins you forgive, they are

forgiven; for those whose sins you retain, they are re-
tained" (John 20:22–23). The traditional understanding
of this text is that Jesus is on this occasion giving all the
apostles a certain power to bind and loose. This has
been seen as the origin of the power that the ordinary
priest or bishop exercises in the ministry of the sacrament of reconciliation. However, I think both of these
texts can in some way be truly applied to every disciple
of Christ. We are all called to be ministers of reconciliation, ministers of Christ's forgiveness in our daily for-
giving of one another and of our enemies and of ourselves. The compassion of any disciple's heart is a
channel through which Christ's healing, redeeming,
and reconciling grace can flow. The hardness of any
disciple's heart that withholds forgiveness in some way
blocks the grace of God's forgiveness from reaching the
hearts of our brothers and sisters.

*   *   *

As we walk with Peter we see a very weak and fearful
man who hides consistently behind the defensiveness
of boasting and bravado and who quakes before the
challenge of a little serving-girl. We will, though, see
this man, in fulfillment of the prophetic naming of the
Lord, become a true *Rock* who will without hesitation
withstand the threats of imprisonment and be ready to
be led where he would prefer not to go. What made the
difference? The *Resurrection.* The grace of the Resurrection given to Peter by Christ and brought to fullness
by the outpouring of the Holy Spirit enabled this very
weak, imperfect human being to become a powerful
and empowering disciple. The folly and the victory of

Peter can give all of us disciples of Christ cause to hope that we too can enter into the mystery of Resurrection and experience in our lives that same transforming grace.

Resurrection

The spirit in the upper room was very different from
what it was some forty days before. Then Jesus had
disappeared from their midst, led away by a cohort, and
less than twenty-four hours later he was hidden behind
the stone slab that covered the door of a tomb. Then
the disciples cowered in the upper room, fearful and
uncertain—those that hadn't headed out of the city like
the two on their way to Emmaus. Forty-three days later
Jesus departed again from their midst, this time
through a glorious ascension. As he went he left them
with a command and a promise. They were now in the
upper room, in obedience to that command, and filled
with the expectation of the promise.

Gathered with Mary, the mother of Jesus, whom he
had bequeathed to the whole Church—"Behold your
mother"—they were engaged in a final preparation for
the epiphany of the Church.

Jesus had spent much of his lifetime in preparation,
living an ordinary life in the obscure town of Nazareth.
His immediate preparation for his public ministry was
forty days spent apart in prayer. Again and again he
nourished his ministry with time apart, especially at
night in solitary prayer to the Father. On various occasions he asked chosen ones to be with him, as on Tabor

and in Gethsemane. Now the disciples, following the example of the Master, were preparing for a promised event with a period of apartness in prayer—"Go into your room, close your door, and pray to your Father in secret" (Matthew 6:6).

After ten days of preparation the Spirit came upon the disciples in power. It was now time for Simon, who had truly become Peter, the Rock, to stand forth with power and proclaim the Resurrection of the Lord Jesus: "Men of Israel, listen to what I am going to say: Jesus the Nazarene was a man commended to you by God by the miracles and portents and signs that God worked through him when he was among you, as you all know. This man, who was put into your power by the deliberate intention and foreknowledge of God, you took and had crucified by men outside the Law. You killed him, but God raised him to life" (Acts 2:22–23).

We cannot help being astonished. Here—probably in the very Temple itself, for such a large group of Christians—120 of them—could not have readily found room in any other "house" in Jerusalem; but the porticoes of the Temple would have been available to them, and the large crowd of Jews in the courts of the Temple could then easily perceive the powerful coming of the Spirit—here stands the man who quaked before the simple interrogation of a servant girl; now he boldly proclaims the very things for which his Master was put to death less than two months before. And he didn't mince his words, either.

The proclamation of the fact of the Resurrection of the Lord Jesus would become central in all the teaching of Peter. When he performed his first public healing in the Temple he declared openly: "God, however, raised him from the dead, and of that fact we are the witnesses; and it is the name of Jesus which, through our faith in it, has brought back the strength of this man whom you see here and who is well known to you. It is faith in that name that has restored this man to health, as you can see" (Acts 3:15–16). When he was brought before the Sanhedrin, he told them, "It was the God of our ancestors who raised up Jesus, but it was you who had him executed by hanging on a tree. By his own right hand God has now raised him up to be leader and savior, to give repentance and forgiveness of sins through him to Israel. We are witnesses to all this, we and the Holy Spirit whom God has given to those who obey him" (Acts 5:30–32).

And when he was called to give witness to the Gentiles: "Now I, and those with me, can witness to everything that Jesus did throughout the countryside of Judaea and Jerusalem itself; and also to the fact that they killed him by hanging him on a tree, yet three days afterwards God raised him to life and allowed him to be seen, not by the whole people but only by certain witnesses God had chosen beforehand" (Acts 10:39–41).

Fearlessly Peter went forth to proclaim the Resurrection of the Lord Jesus Christ, his Master. So far as we know he was never laughed to scorn, as was Paul, but he was jailed (Acts 4:3) and flogged (Acts 5:40) and eventually "led where he would not go" and crucified. Jesus had prepared Peter carefully step by step to be able fully to understand and integrate the meaning and the power of the Resurrection.

One of the first steps was that day when Jesus came

into Peter's home and raised his mother-in-law from her sick bed. Peter witnessed Jesus' power of resurrection again when he was one of the chosen witnesses at the restoration of Jairus' daughter:

> While he was still speaking, someone arrived from the house of the synagogue official to say, "Your daughter has died. Do not trouble the Master any further." But Jesus had heard this, and he spoke to the man, "Do not be afraid, only have faith and she will be safe." When he came to the house he allowed no one to go in with him except Peter and John and James, and the child's father and mother. They were all weeping and mourning for her, but Jesus said, "Stop crying; she is not dead, but asleep." But they laughed at him, knowing she was dead. But taking her by the hand he called to her, "Child, get up." And her spirit returned and she got up at once. Then he told them to give her something to eat. [Luke 8:49–55]

The mourners outside laughed Jesus to scorn when he said she was only asleep. Perhaps later Peter himself would have wondered whether that was indeed the case. But the experience at Nain was even stronger and clearer, for here there could seem to be no doubt about the death of the young man who was already being carried to the cemetery:

> Now soon afterwards he went to a town called Nain, accompanied by his disciples and a great number of people. When he was near the gate of the town it happened that a dead man was being

carried out for burial, the only son of his mother,
and she was a widow. And a considerable number
of the townspeople were with her. When the Lord
saw her he felt sorry for her. "Do not cry," he said.
Then he went up and put his hand on the bier and
the bearers stood still, and he said, "Young man, I
tell you to get up." And the dead man sat up and
began to talk, and Jesus gave him to his mother.
[Luke 7:11–15]

If any question still lurked in Peter's heart, raised by
the skeptics who would have said that somehow the lad
of Nain was really only in some deep coma and not
truly dead, all such skepticism would have been dissipated with the experience of Lazarus:

Jesus said in great distress, with a sigh that came
straight from the heart, "Where have you put
him?" They said, "Lord, come and see." Jesus
wept; and the Jews said, "See how much he loved
him!" But there were some who remarked, "He
opened the eyes of the blind man, could he not
have prevented this man's death?" Still sighing,
Jesus reached the tomb: it was a cave with a stone
to close the opening. Jesus said, "Take the stone
away." Martha said to him, "Lord, by now he will
smell; this is the fourth day." Jesus replied, "Have I
not told you that if you believe you will see the
glory of God?" So they took away the stone. Then
Jesus lifted up his eyes and said:

Father: I thank you for hearing my prayer.
I knew indeed that you always hear me,

but I speak
for the sake of all these who stand round me,
so that they may believe it was you who sent
me.

When he had said this, he cried in a loud voice,
"Lazarus, here! Come out!" The dead man came
out, his feet and hands bound with bands of stuff
and a cloth round his face. Jesus said to them,
"Unbind him, let him go free." [John 11:33–44]

After such experiences it was not so difficult, even
though the apostles generally took the story of the
women as "pure nonsense and they did not believe
them," for Peter to run with hope to an empty tomb.
We will never know the details, not to speak of the
inner emotions experienced by Peter, in that moment
when he did indeed encounter his Risen Lord.

Peter internalized the meaning and the power of the
grace of the Resurrection. And when the occasion
came, with the courage of a true disciple he did not
hesitate to call upon the power of his Master.

At Jaffa there was a woman disciple called Tabitha, or Dorcas in Greek, who never tired of doing
good or giving in charity. But the time came when
she got ill and died, and they washed her and laid
her out in a room upstairs. Lydda is not far from
Jaffa, so when the disciples heard that Peter was
there, they sent two men with an urgent message
for him: "Come and visit us as soon as possible."

Peter went back with them straightaway, and on
his arrival they took him to the upstairs room,

where all the widows stood round him in tears,
showing him tunics and the other clothes which
Dorcas had made when she was with them. Peter
sent them all out of the room and knelt down and
prayed. Then he turned to the dead woman and
said, "Tabitha, stand up." She opened her eyes,
looked at Peter and sat up. Peter helped her to her
feet, then called in the saints and widows and
showed them she was alive. [Acts 9:36–41]

When we compare this scene with that which took
place in the house of Jairus, we see very much the disciple in the shadow of his Master—just as when we look
back in the Old Testament we see in Elijah the Prophet
the foreshadowing of what was to come. But there is
this great difference both in the case of Elijah and of
Peter: the Prophet and the Disciple, before bringing the
grace of the Resurrection, had to kneel in prayer and
call upon the Lord; while the Master simply stretched
forth his hand and called the child to life.

In his old age, Peter would write from Rome, fully
conscious "that the time for taking off this tent is coming soon, as the Lord Jesus Christ had foretold" (2 Peter 1:14). After greeting the Christians who had been
scattered to all parts of the Dispersion, he immediately
proclaimed with gratitude the essence of the good
news: "Blessed be God the Father of our Lord Jesus
Christ, who in his great mercy has given us a new birth
as his sons, by raising Jesus Christ from the dead, so
that we have a sure hope and promise of an inheritance
that can never be spoilt or soiled and never fade away,

because it is being kept for you in the heavens" (1 Peter 1:3–4).

Peter himself had come to know how certain is the hope that he found in the Resurrection of Jesus Christ. That hope cannot be spoiled or soiled in spite of human frailty and weakness, stupidity and blundering. It was a power that could even raise the dead. But Peter knew, too, that he was able to live out the power of the Resurrection and proclaim it fearlessly only after he had received the Spirit. It is not enough to know, not even enough to experience. Knowledge and experience have to become in us a living, effective knowledge through the grace and empowerment of the Holy Spirit. Then we can continually rise from our failures and our weakness, and we can help others to rise from theirs; then we can live worthily as disciples of a Risen Master.

The Resurrection must be central in the life and thinking of a disciple of Christ, not only as the source of all that he is but as the primary proclamation of his life. If we do not live as men and women who believe in the Resurrection, we are not true disciples of Christ. If we do not bring to others the message of hope that is the Resurrection, we fail them and our Master. Christ is risen! Yes, he is truly risen.

Restoration

Later on, Jesus showed himself to his disciples. It was by the sea of Tiberias, and it happened like this: Simon Peter, Thomas called the Twin, Nathanael from Cana in Galilee, the sons of Zebedee and two more of his disciples were together. Simon Peter said, "I'm going fishing." They replied, "We'll come with you." They went out and got into the boat but caught nothing that night.

It was light by now and there stood Jesus on the shore, though the disciples did not realize that it was Jesus. Jesus called out, "Have you caught anything, friends?" And when they answered, "No," he said, "Throw the net out to starboard and you'll find something." So they dropped the net, and there were so many fish that they could not haul it in. The disciple Jesus loved said to Peter, "It is the Lord." At these words, "It is the Lord," Simon Peter, who had practically nothing on, wrapped his cloak around him and jumped into the water. The other disciples came on in the boat, towing the net and the fish; they were only about a hundred yards from land.

As soon as they came ashore they saw that there was some bread there, and a charcoal fire with fish cooking on it. Jesus said, "Bring some of the fish you have just caught." Simon Peter went aboard and dragged the net to the shore, full of big fish, one hundred and fifty-three of them; and in spite of there being so many the net was not broken. Jesus said to them, "Come and have breakfast." None of the disciples was bold enough to ask, "Who are you?"; they knew quite well that it was the Lord. Jesus then stepped forward, took the bread and gave it to them, and the same with the fish. This was the third time that Jesus showed himself to the disciples after rising from the dead.

After the meal Jesus said to Simon Peter, "Simon son of John, do you love me more than these others do?" He answered, "Yes, Lord, you know that I love you." Jesus said to him, "Feed my lambs." A second time he said to him, "Simon son of John, do you love me?" He replied, "Yes, Lord, you know I love you." Jesus said to him, "Look after my sheep." Then he said to him a third time, "Simon son of John, do you love me?" Peter was upset that he asked him the third time, "Do you love me?" and said, "Lord, you know everything; you know that I love you." Jesus said to him, "Feed my sheep.

I tell you most solemnly,
when you were young
you put on your own belt
and walked where you liked;
but when you grow old
you will stretch out your hands,

and somebody else will put a belt around you
and take you where you would rather not go."

In these words he indicated the kind of death by
which Peter would give glory to God. After this he
said, "Follow me." [John 21:1–19]

Peter had denied Christ three times. Caught up in the
swirl of the emotions of the moment, he acted out of
reaction; he reacted rather than acting from his own
true, deep self. The glance of Jesus, who understood all
only too well, was much more a look of compassion,
love, and pity than one of rebuke. It was enough to
bring Peter back to his true self. He went out and wept
bitterly.

We know nothing of the encounter of Peter with
Jesus on Easter, but it certainly restored the very special bond of love that existed between Master and Disciple. Once again, Peter was fully a disciple of Jesus.
But the wise Master would restore him to his very particular role of apostolic ministry and leadership only
step by step.

At first he left Peter and the others waiting; only
occasionally would he come to them. Prayer is often a
matter of waiting. We go to prayer each day. But oftentimes the Lord doesn't seem to show up. Actually, of
course, he is there, or we wouldn't be there. Only by his
grace do we seek him in prayer. It is only by his grace
that we wait for him. This waiting is important because
it develops in us an ever-deeper longing for him. We
come to know more and more in the depths of our
being our need for him and how he is the center, the
meaning of all our life. It is important that we be faith-

ful to this daily waiting. For we do not know just when he will come.

Yet in the midst of this waiting, ordinary life must go on. So Peter decided to go back to his nets. Natural leader of the group that he was, he drew the others after him.

Oftentimes in our lives we have a sense of not really knowing what God does want of us. We know we want to serve him, and serve him perhaps in a special and wholehearted way, but it just isn't clear what he wants right now. Then the only thing to do is as Peter did, go fishing. Go about the daily duties of life. If God wants something else, it is his responsibility to come and find us there—that is where he will expect to find us—and let us know what he wants.

And so Peter and his friends went back to their boats and their nets. And it was there that Jesus found them. Or rather, it might be more correct to say that it was there that Jesus turned up, and they found him.

The second step in the restoration of Peter renews, as it were, his call to apostolic mission. And it is similar to the previous call, as it is described in Saint Luke's account.

Jesus said to Simon, "Put out into deep water and pay out your nets for a catch." "Master," Simon replied, "we worked hard all night long and caught nothing, but if you say so, I will pay out the nets." And when they had done this they netted such a huge number of fish that their nets began to tear, so they signaled to their companions in the other boat to come and help them; when these came, they filled the two boats to the sinking point.

When Simon Peter saw this he fell at the knees of Jesus saying, "Leave me, Lord; I am a sinful man." For he and all his companions were completely overcome by the catch they had made; so also were James and John, the sons of Zebedee, who were Simon's partners. But Jesus said to Simon, "Do not be afraid, from now on it is men you will catch." Then, bringing their boats back to land, they left everything and followed him. [Luke 5:4–11]

There is a directness and openness in this earlier call that is somewhat obscured in the restoration. A certain obtuseness seems to veil Peter's eyes. He does not recognize the stranger on the shore. And even in the moment of the miraculous draught of fishes he does not yet come to realization by himself. This is so true of ourselves. How often, even though we are really seeking the Lord, and seeking to do his will, yet there is a part in us that is reluctant to see him here and now. Perhaps it is because in the call and the response to it there is always necessarily a conversion, an acknowledgment that the past has not been all that it should have been. Perhaps too there is something in us that does not want to respond to the call for the further gift of self. The false self is hanging on to its established ways, the familiar ways where it is most comfortable. It took John, the pure, the innocent, with the keen eyes of love, to perceive that the "Friend" on the shore was indeed the Lord: "It is the Lord."

This is one of the reasons why we have such great need of a spiritual guide or friend in our lives. I don't particularly care for the term "spiritual director," for I believe that the only one who can direct is the one who truly knows in fullness that to which we are called. That is the Holy Spirit himself. He is the true director of our lives. The role of the spiritual guide or friend is to help us to hear what the Lord is saying, to see what he is doing in our lives. It was John who saw that it was Jesus, and that Jesus was now calling Peter to himself.

Peter had undergone a true reconversion to Christ. So there was no hesitation in his response once he clearly perceived the call. Yet there was a certain reverence for the Lord. This man, who had acted with such presumption that once it even called forth from the Lord the rebuke, "Get behind me, Satan," now would not appear before his Lord without properly clothing himself, even though it would indeed be cumbersome as he plunged into the water and went pell-mell with all his old enthusiasm to the feet of his Master. Here Peter shows again in graphic image his willingness to leave everything: friends, boat, prosperous income—he leaves it all in order to respond to Jesus.

The other disciples came following after, laboriously pulling the weighted ship up onto the shore until it was nestled securely in the sands. The one who has left everything behind to respond to Christ can with alacrity plunge ahead to be with him. However, the vocation of those disciples who have not been called to evangelical poverty is also very important. The Church needs the material wherewithal that they bring to her service.

Jesus with his usual graciousness had prepared a breakfast for his disciples. With great delicacy and sacramental significance, he invites Peter to play a part in providing this meal: "Bring some of the fish you have just caught." Simon in his enthusiasm doesn't bring just some of the fish. He grabs the net and single-handed brings the entire catch to the feet of the Lord. The uniqueness of Peter's role in the Church is again symbolized. However, equally symbolic is the fact that it was the community of disciples that had made available to Peter the means to serve the Lord and carry out his ministry in such fullness.

Peter stood there beaming. He was proud of himself and of what he had just accomplished. He had been able to display his strength and his command of the situation. Jesus knew the inherent dangers in accomplished and forceful leadership. So again, as at the Last Supper, he, the Lord and Master, gave the example. He quietly went about the humble tasks of cook and server. He turned the fish on the coals, made sure the bread was done, and then with his own hands he served each of his disciples the fresh-baked bread and the roasted fish. As the Lord served Peter, some of the same emotions that welled up at the Last Supper, when the Master knelt at his feet, again stirred in his breast. But Peter had learned. He knew he had to be served, nourished, and cared for by the Master if he himself was going to be able not only to be a disciple but also to serve the other disciples in the stead of the Master. Peter was ready to be restored to apostolic leadership. For many of us, especially those of us whose lives are about ministry, it is oftentimes very difficult to let others, and even the Lord himself, minister to us. But no one can minister well if he has not first been ministered unto. The best nurses are those who have been patients. The best superiors were good subjects. A good spiritual father always has a spiritual father.

After the meal was complete, Jesus looked Peter in the eye and said very simply and very directly, "Simon son of John, do you love me more than these others do?" It was a very testing question indeed. For Jesus didn't simply ask, "Do you love me?" but "Do you love me more than these others do?" Simon was being called to a special role, a special responsibility within the apostolic community of disciples. A wiser, humbler Peter answered, "Yes, Lord, *you know* that I love you." Peter trusted more in Jesus' knowledge of him than in his own knowledge of himself. And Jesus commissioned him, "Feed my lambs." Then he asked him a second time, "Simon son of John, do you love me?" Again Peter answered in the same humble way, "Yes, Lord, you know I love you." And Jesus commissioned him, "Look after my sheep." Tradition has understood the different responses of Jesus here to indicate the commissioning of Peter not only to watch over the lambs—the universal flock of disciples—but also the sheep—those who would be the more mature and responsible disciples, the other shepherds, those called to apostolic ministry.

But then Jesus went on to ask a third time, "Simon son of John, do you love me?" Peter was upset that Jesus asked him a third time. It could not help bringing back to him the fact that, as Jesus had foretold, he had denied Jesus three times. Moreover, the word Jesus used this third time for "love," at least in Saint John's

Greek, is not the one that connotes the preferential love of charity, but rather the personal, human affection that binds together lovers. Jesus was giving Peter the opportunity for complete restoration. Peter was deeply moved. He realized the folly of his presumptuousness at the Last Supper: "Even if I have to die with you, I will never disown you." With great humility and a certain anguish of spirit, realizing his own possible lack of self-knowledge, he cries, "Lord, you know everything; you know that I love you." And again he is commissioned to feed the sheep.

The restoration is now complete. The man who, when caught up in the emotions of the moment and acting out of reaction, had denied the Lord three times, has been called to respond three times from the depths of his being, those depths that we know when we know ourselves in the knowledge of God, a knowledge that is gained only by deep prayer. The man who had been called to be a disciple, to apostolic ministry, and to apostolic leadership was now restored not only to full discipleship and apostolic mission but to his role of apostolic leadership, the responsibility to care not only for the lambs but also for the sheep—the shepherds of the flock.

When we fail the Lord and turn back to him in repentance, his forgiveness is complete and immediate. But as a loving Master and a good pedagogue, he knows that it is far better for us if in some way we have to work at the restoration. And thus his Church has determined that when we have seriously failed the Lord to the extent that our relationship with him has been ruptured and our spiritual life within has been killed, when our sin has been indeed mortal, it is not enough for complete restoration simply to return to the Lord in a personal encounter of repentance and love. We must go through a process of submitting our sinfulness to the ministry of the Church so that we can experience through Christ's minister the laying on of his healing hand and hear the words of pardon and absolution in our ears. If we have received and accepted the call to apostolic mission and then in our weakness have failed and been unfaithful and turned from it, in the time of our repentance we must receive not only the healing forgiveness of Christ but also the absolution of the Church from the censures that we have rightly deserved. These sacramental processes of the Church are not merely outward signs or formalities but graces that help us to experience fully and integrate into our being at every level the fact of our restoration. The Lord who made us knows us through and through, and he knows our need as human beings to experience restoration as fully and integrally as we have experienced our failure and our falls.

With the full restoration of Peter, the apostolic Church was prepared to face the loss of the Master as he ascended on high. It now had a worthy disciple of the Master—one who had been fully chastened by failure and strengthened by the restoring grace of the Resurrection—to accept the responsibilities of leadership in the Church. The Church was now ready for its great epiphany at Pentecost. It was now ready to receive and fulfill the command of its ascending Lord to be "witness not only in Jerusalem but throughout Judaea and Samaria and indeed to the ends of the earth" (Acts 1:8).

The Prophet

Saint Paul has brought out that prophecy is one of the more ordinary gifts that are to be found among the people of God. He lists it along with such gifts as teaching. It is not something as extraordinary as we have tended to think in our more recent history. The popular emphasis on the aspect of prediction of the future has perhaps detracted from the fundamental role of the prophet. His or her role is most properly to proclaim the Lord clearly under the powerful influence of the Holy Spirit. The prophet has had a personal experience of God and interprets this experience in its historical context, and then formulates and articulates that experience for the Christian community. The prophetic word may well address itself to the future, for the call of God in Christ is always a call to that ultimate fullness which is the Kingdom of Heaven. However, in the timelessness of God, that is all "now." "Today, if you hear his voice, harden not your hearts" (Psalm 95:7–8).

When Peter was still acting very much out of his own presumptuous human experience, he proved often enough to be a false prophet. When Jesus foretold for the first time his own passion, death, and resurrection, Peter would have none of it. Later when Jesus foretold Peter's denial, Peter was quick to come forth with his own false prophecy of fidelity even unto death. Happily, in the long run even this prophecy proved to be true.

Peter, very much a man of his times, was interested in prophecy. When Jesus foretold the destruction of the Temple of Jerusalem it was Peter, as spokesman for the others, who asked the Lord, "Tell us when is this going to happen, what sign will there be that all this is about to be fulfilled." When they gathered on Olivet for the leave-taking of the Lord it was the Spokesman of the Twelve who again gave voice to the question that was in the minds of all: "Lord, has the time come? Are you going to restore the Kingdom of Israel?" Jesus replied, "It is not for you to know the times or dates that the Father has decided by his own authority" (Acts 1:6–7). Peter heard this well and kept it in mind. Later, as pastor of the Churches, he would remind all the flock of the Lord that "with the Lord, a day can mean a thousand years, and a thousand years is like a day" (2 Peter 3:8). The time element of a prophecy is not the important thing. Peter, as the universal shepherd, would try to help correct some of the misapprehensions that came from Paul's prophecies of the end times (2 Peter 3:15–16).

If the important thing in prophecy, then, is not the time element, what is? The really important thing is the clear and powerful witness to the ultimate fulfillment of all things in Christ Jesus. When Peter comes into his own with the coming of the Holy Spirit and begins to speak out powerfully in his first discourse in the Temple, he not only gives a prophetic word, he identifies himself with the great prophets of God who went before:

> Now you must repent and turn to God, so that
> your sins may be wiped out, and so that the Lord
> may send the time of comfort. Then he will send
> you the Christ that he has predestined, that is
> Jesus, whom heaven must keep till the universal
> restoration comes which God proclaimed, speaking
> through his holy prophets. Moses, for example,
> said: *The Lord God will raise up a prophet like my-*
> *self for you, from among your own brothers; you must*
> *listen to whatever he tells you. The man who does not*
> *listen to that prophet is to be cut off from the people.*
> In fact, all the prophets that have ever spoken,
> from Samuel onwards, have predicted these days.
> [Acts 3:19–24]

As an old man writing his final word to the Churches,
Peter continues in this same prophetic vein:

> You did not see him, yet you love him; and still
> without seeing him, you are already filled with a
> joy so glorious that it cannot be described, because
> you believe; and you are sure of the end to which
> your faith looks forward, that is, the salvation of
> your souls.
>
> It was this salvation that the prophets were
> looking and searching so hard for; their prophecies
> were about the grace which was to come to you.
> The Spirit of Christ which was in them foretold
> the sufferings of Christ and the glories that would
> come after them, and they tried to find out at what

time and in what circumstances all this was to be expected. It was revealed to them that the news they brought of all the things which have now been announced to you, by those who preached to you the Good News through the Holy Spirit sent from heaven, was for you and not for themselves. Even the angels long to catch a glimpse of these things. [1 Peter 1:8–12]

That Spirit lodges in the heart of every disciple of Christ and proclaims powerfully to him, and invites him to proclaim to others, the coming fullness, the sure hope we have in the Lord Jesus as our Master, and in our fidelity to him.

However, Peter gives us a wise precautionary note in regard to the prophetic spirit that lies within us: "You will be right to depend on prophecy and take it as a lamp for lighting a way through the dark until the dawn comes and the morning star rises in your minds. At the same time, we must be most careful to remember that the interpretation of scriptural prophecy is never a matter for the individual. Why? Because no prophecy ever came from man's initiative. When men spoke for God it was the Holy Spirit that moved them" (2 Peter 1:19–21).

The sureness of prophecy comes from its adherence to the common teaching and expectations of the whole Christian community. Any prophetic word that is at odds with such teaching is not authentic.

We do find in the final words of Peter a prophecy that speaks with a special power to us in our times. For it seems to be a clear prophecy of that which we dread, a nuclear holocaust. "By the same word, the present sky and earth are destined for fire . . . The Day of the Lord will come like a thief, and then with a roar the sky will vanish, the elements will catch fire and fall apart, the earth and all that it contains will be burnt up. . . . the sky will dissolve in flames and the elements melt in the heat" (2 Peter 3:7–12).

But Peter goes immediately on to say, "What we are waiting for is what he promised: the new heavens and new earth, the place where righteousness will be at home" (2 Peter 3:13). As terrible as is the prophecy of such a holocaust—and we can hope and pray that it will be averted by our due conversion and repentance— yet it is the role of the true disciple of Christ to bring hope that can go even beyond nuclear holocaust. Whether this earth is to be destroyed by fire or not, we know that in the end the transforming power of Christ will prevail, and there will be "new heavens and a new earth."

The function of the prophet may all too often be an unpopular one of speaking the truth in justice and calling to repentance. We can remember how poor Jonah, when called to such a prophetic mission, took a boat and sailed in the opposite direction. It was only by most extraordinary interventions of Providence that he was brought back to his prophetic task. We can also remember how fruitful was his prophetic word. It brought a city to repentance and salvation. By speaking out of the fullness of the truth that we have received in the experience of the risen Christ, we can bring the greatest hope our world has to escape the holocaust. It is only when we learn to put our trust in the Lord our God rather than in the false idols of arms and nuclear weapons that we can hope to come to a new fellowship among the children of God which will enable us to lay aside our arms and build together, in trust, a human community that will indeed under God create "new heavens and a new earth."

The challenge to us as disciples of Christ in our prophetic role is to discern how we can not only enter fully into this perspective but so live it that our lives are a clear prophetic witness to our fellows. Each of us under the guidance of the Spirit and the ecclesial community will be led to that witness which is appropriate to us in our particular roles among the people of God. While we seek to live out our Gospel witness for peace and the Kingdom of God, we will need to trust and support our brothers and sisters and respect their particular witness even if it is quite different from ours and perhaps difficult for us to understand. All true disciples of Christ are bonded in a common concern for peace on earth and good will among the children of the Father. In this community of concern we have a bonding far deeper and more significant than any of the differences we perceive in the way we concretely express this concern. The multiple expressions only ensure that all persons of good will can receive the common witness of the disciples of Christ, the Prince of Peace.

The Cost of Discipleship

To put it very simply and directly, the cost of discipleship is nothing less than everything, all that we are and all that we have. A disciple to be a true disciple must bring to his Master his whole self and all the potential of his life. Jesus had said very explicitly, "If anyone wants to be a follower of mine, let him renounce himself and take up his cross every day and follow me" (Luke 9:23). We don't take up that cross just to carry it, but to be with Christ crucified on it. He did say, "A man can have no greater love than to lay down his life for his friends" (John 15:13). But he gave us a new commandment—not a counsel, not a bit of advice—but a commandment: "Love one another as I have loved you." And how did he love us? He loved us to the extent of giving his very life for us. To fulfull the commandment of Christ, to be his disciples, we must give our whole selves to him, and to each other for love of him, to do always the things that please the Father.

When Peter wrote to "all those living among the foreigners in the Dispersion of Pontus, Galatia, Cappadocia, Asia and Bithynia," he told them that they would "for a short time have to bear to be plagued with all sorts of trials" (1 Peter 1:6). He knew whereof he spoke. He knew that faith has to be "tested and proved like gold" (1 Peter 1:7). He had before himself the example of Christ: "He was insulted and did not retaliate with insults; when he was tortured he made no threats" (1 Peter 2:23). "Anyone who in this life has bodily suffering has broken with sin, because for the rest of his life on earth he is not ruled by human passions but only by the will of God" (1 Peter 4:1–2).

> My dear people, you must not think it unaccountable that you should be tested by fire. There is nothing extraordinary in what has happened to you. If you can have some share in the sufferings of Christ, be glad, because you will enjoy a much greater gladness when his glory is revealed. It is a blessing for you when they insult you for bearing the name of Christ, because it means that you have the Spirit of glory, the Spirit of God resting on you. . . . If anyone of you should suffer for being a Christian, then he is not to be ashamed of it; he should thank God that he has been called one. [1 Peter 4:12–16]

This is the way of true discipleship.

Discipleship certainly cost Peter. It cost him a settled home and family. "The Son of Man has nowhere to lay his head" (Luke 9:58). When Peter accepted the invitation to follow his Master, he too no longer had whereon to lay his head.

It cost Peter his illusions and his self-pretence. How often do we hear the disciples bickering among themselves as to who is the greatest, who should have the first place, who should sit at the right and the left of the Lord. And Jesus cut through all of that by example and

the affirmation that he who is the greatest should be
among his brethren as the very least. When Peter was
so pretentious as even to rebuff the Master, he was
quickly put in his place as being one of Satan's. When
he had the audacity to speak for the Master when he
was not properly authorized to do so, he was simply
told to "go fish." When he was so cocksure about his
loyalty, he had to hear a cock chant his weakness, the
signal for a loving glance that would burn into his very
heart and bring forth searing tears that would burn
their way down his cheeks, bringing about the cauteri-
zation of his pride and a conversion to a new life.

Discipleship cost Peter his freedom. More than once
he would know the darkness of sitting in a prison cell.

> They arrested them [Peter and John], but as it
> was already late, they held them till the next day.
> [Acts 4:3]

> Then the high priest intervened with all his sup-
> porters from the party of the Sadducees.
> Prompted by jealousy, they arrested the apostles
> and had them put in the common jail. [Acts 5:17–
> 18]

> It was about this time that King Herod started
> persecuting certain members of the Church. He
> beheaded James the brother of John, and when he
> saw that this pleased the Jews he decided to arrest
> Peter as well. This was during the days of Unleav-
> ened Bread, and he put Peter in prison, assigning
> four squads of four soldiers each to guard him in
> turns. Herod meant to try Peter in public after the
> end of Passover week. All the time Peter was un-

der guard the Church prayed to God for him unre-
mittingly.

On the night before Herod was to try him, Peter
was sleeping between two soldiers, fastened with
double chains, while guards kept watch at the
main entrance to the prison. Then suddenly the
angel of the Lord stood there, and the cell was
filled with light. He tapped Peter on the side and
woke him. "Get up!" he said, "Hurry!"—the chains
fell from his hands. The angel then said, "Put on
your belt and sandals." After he had done this, the
angel next said, "Wrap your cloak round you and
follow me." Peter followed him, but had no idea
that what the angel did was all happening in reality; he thought he was seeing a vision. They passed
through two guard posts one after the other and
reached the iron gate leading to the city. This
opened of its own accord; they went through it
and had walked the whole length of one street
when suddenly the angel left him. It was only then
that Peter came to himself. "Now I know it is all
true," he said. "The Lord did really send his angel
and has saved me from Herod and from all that
the Jewish people were so certain would happen to
me."

As soon as he realized this he went straight to
the house of Mary the mother of John Mark,
where a number of people had assembled and
were praying. He knocked at the outside door and
a servant called Rhoda came to answer it. She recognized Peter's voice and was so overcome with
joy that, instead of opening the door, she ran in-

side with the news that Peter was standing at the main entrance. They said to her, "You are out of your mind," but she insisted that it was true. Then they said, "It must be an angel!" Peter, meanwhile, was still knocking, so they opened the door and were amazed to see that it really was Peter himself. With a gesture of his hand he stopped them talking, and described to them how the Lord had led him out of prison. He added, "Tell James and the brothers." Then he left and went to another place. [Acts 12:1–17]

We can imagine how Peter was feeling at this time. James had been his companion, his fellow worker, his partner on the Sea of Galilee, and his partner in the adventures of life. Together they had gone to seek and search. They had found John the Baptizer. Then they found Christ. Now James was gone. He had been cruelly beheaded. Then Peter was seized, and there was no doubt about what the plans were in his regard. Have you ever thought how it would feel to sit hour after hour, contemplating the fact that you were shortly to have your head cut off? Peter knew the experience of death row. Disciples live there, too.

In addition, to make matters worse, it was the great Feast of Passover. Everyone outside, at least so it seemed to one peering out through prison bars, was rejoicing, celebrating the feast. Life was going on at a high point. And here was Peter left alone in his cell with no one, it seemed, caring the least about his fate. He was not quite alone. A couple of times already by miraculous intervention he had escaped from a prison cell. This time Herod was taking no chances. He had Peter chained, he had guards posted all over the place. As Peter sat there, his situation seemed desperate indeed.

Sometimes God lets us get pushed completely into a corner, into what seems to be an absolutely hopeless situation, before he steps forward to help us. He does this so that we might more fully realize our need of his help. He is the source of salvation—we can't do it ourselves. In the case of Lazarus, the sisters sent word to Jesus in good time that the brother whom they and he loved was sick (John 11:3). But Jesus tarried in coming. If he healed Lazarus before he died, people could say that his own natural resources had brought him back to good health. If Jesus raised him from dead almost immediately after he died, they could say the death was an illusion; he was only in a deep coma, and Jesus roused him. And so Jesus tarried, and the situation became completely hopeless. "Lord, by now he will smell; this is the fourth day" (John 11:39). Only then did he say to Lazarus, "Come forth!" All saw the glory of God.

If the Lord had kept Peter from getting caught and imprisoned, Peter might have thought that he had eluded his persecutors by using his own natural talents and abilities. Being in prison, reduced to a state of hopelessness, then indeed he, and everyone else, saw that liberation comes from the Lord.

The ultimate release and healing is that of eternal life. In our shortsightedness we do not always see that. We think that the Lord must always come to our rescue here on earth. God has heaven and all eternity in which to respond to the deep aspirations of our prayer. When it seems he is allowing things to deteriorate to their very worst—Peter ultimately was crucified—God is still going to right it all. He will respond to all our deepest aspirations raised to him in confident prayer in the ultimate victory in the Kingdom of Heaven.

For the moment, Peter was free. He hastened to the home of friends. Perhaps this was the same house in which they celebrated the Last Supper and where they sought to hide after the crucifixion. In any case, Peter was not mistaken, there were friends there. "A number of people had assembled and were praying." We see a very agitated Peter, eager to get off the streets, eager to be embraced by the love of the community, pounding feverishly at that door. The prayer inside was going strong and it took time for anyone to hear him. Finally someone did hear, and a servant-girl was sent to see who was there. She recognized Peter's voice, but in her excitement, instead of opening the door and letting the poor man in, she ran to tell everybody that Peter was there. And Peter continued to stand outside, pounding and pounding fruitlessly against the unyielding door, while the people inside, who held him in such love, incredulously debated the meaning of the pounding. Peter experienced here, even if only momentarily, what is often the fate of those who are called to exercise their discipleship through the service of responsibility and leadership. All too often, those who are called to leadership are left out of the warmth of the community. Leaders, carrying the heaviest burdens and most in need of support, are somehow seen to be beyond the ordinary everyday support of the community of brethren. Indeed, they often have to bear the brunt of failing to live up to exaggerated standards that the community sets for them, and they are expected to bear this and everything else with equanimity.

One day I had the privilege of sitting in on a dialogue between one of our Cistercian abbots and a Buddhist abbot from a monastery in Thailand. They were sharing their experiences of the service of abbatial responsibility and authority. The wise old Buddhist abbot, whose name was Achincha, queried the Cistercian abbot: "Do you know what is a superior? Do you know what is an abbot?" "No, what is an abbot?" said the gracious host, giving his guest the space to make the declaration he obviously wanted to set forth. "An abbot is a garbage collector. He is the one into whose lap the brethren can dump all their garbage. And he will carry it away for them."

All too often the Christian community surrounds its leaders with respect, veneration, and a caring love that is expressed in prayer—but unfortunately not expressed in human warmth, compassion, and solidarity. The one who is called to leadership must accept his role and accept this reality. He may do what he can to change it. He may have to create elsewhere the support he needs. But ultimately, in his lonely role as superior or leader, he must find his all in Christ, for whom and in whose name he serves.

At last the door did open and Peter was admitted into the warmth of the community. He could only remain momentarily; he did not want to endanger them. After sharing with them the good news of the powerful intervention of the angel of the Lord—Peter must have relished every detail of the escape—he had to slip away into hiding and exile.

In his discipleship Peter did find a new, deeper freedom that perdured even in the midst of imprisonment and exile. And even in death. But as he found this freedom he found another kind of enslavement, the most beautiful kind there is, the enslavement of love. When we truly love someone, when we truly become the disciple of the Master, our whole life can only be a "yes" to the Beloved. And thus discipleship cost Peter his life.

> I tell you most solemnly,
> when you were young
> you put on your own belt
> and walked where you liked;
> but when you grow old
> you will stretch out your hands,
> and somebody else will put a belt around you
> and take you where you would rather not go.

In these words Jesus indicated the kind of death by which Peter would give glory to God. After this he said, "Follow me." [John 21:18–19]

In his younger days Peter did what he wanted, but in truth he was the slave of his own fears, his own false ego, his own defensiveness and bravado. In his old age, when he came into freedom from all these things, freedom indeed from himself, he became the slave of love. And out of love for his Master he would stretch forth his hands and be led forth from imprisonment to the cross. The man who once was so presumptuous as to rebuke his Master and try to tell him what he should do and how he should behave, in his love had grown so humble that he did not even feel worthy to die as his Master had died. Tradition tells us that in that last hour he begged his executioners to crucify him upside down. Thus Peter hung, and saw with full clarity that as disciples of Christ, our feet are planted in the heavens and everything hangs from the mercy of God.

Epilogue

There is certainly much more that can be said about Peter as a disciple and as a master of discipleship. We have only looked at those texts that specifically speak about Peter, and not even all of them. Any of the texts that speak about the disciples or the apostles as a group will ordinarily include Peter. My primary intention here has been to introduce the perception of Peter as one to whom we can turn to learn how to be good disciples of our Master. He is a model and an inspiration. But he can be more than that.

Peter can be a living teacher. For Peter certainly is not dead; he is very much alive in the Lord. In faith we can come to him and sit with him and let him speak to us through the Scriptures and through the communion of prayer. He can intercede for us in his own prayer, obtaining for us the grace we need to be true and worthy disciples of our common Master, the Lord Jesus.

A few years ago I had the privilege of walking along the shores of the Sea of Galilee. As I looked at the many fishermen there working in their boats or mending their nets or sorting their catch and loading them onto trucks, I wondered how many of them have the same potential as Peter. Any passerby on the shores of the Sea of Galilee in the year 30 would have seen Peter as just one more of the fishermen. He had certain outstanding qualities. He was in some ways an exceptional human being. And yet in the end, if he was outstanding, he was just an outstanding fisherman. He remained a fisherman of the Sea of Galilee.

For a moment, let us turn our glance back upon ourselves. How do others see us? One more worker going about the ordinary everyday task. Oh yes, we have our own particular outstanding qualities. We may be one of the best of our class—but we are still one of the class. Is that what we really want? Is that the way we want to live out our discipleship? Many of the disciples of Jesus, after accepting him as Master, go back to their everyday tasks. They do them with a new depth of understanding and vision. Others working beside them may remark a change; they may be invited to discover its deeper meaning, invited to join them in discipleship. This is the more usual, and a very valid way to follow Christ, to be his disciple. The call to discipleship does not always mean leaving one's home, family, goods, and daily concerns. Rather, it means bringing to them a Presence, a new Spirit.

However, the choice is ours. The Lord does invite all those who wish so to respond to him, to a fuller discipleship in the practice of those qualities of life that have been traditionally called the evangelical counsels. We can embrace a life of more complete obedience to the Lord, committing ourselves to a particular service. We can embrace a new freedom in following the Lord by giving up our possessions and living from the common sharing of the Christian community. We can find a special freedom to be to the Lord by forgoing a home and a family of our own so that the attachment of our life is an attachment to the Lord Jesus, in his love embracing the whole Christian community and the whole human family. We may want to live out these qualities of life as we embrace the Master in the contemplative way of life. We may want to reach out to others and share in the apostolic ministry. To the full practice of the evangelical councils many are called—the Lord gives witness—but few choose this way. Sometimes what holds back young men and women, or older men and women who are thinking of a second or third career, from stepping forward and choosing to follow the Lord in such a relationship is a sense of unworthiness or inadequacy. Our contact with Peter will help us to realize that this is no reason at all. We have such a Master that even the most inadequate, the weakest, the most stupid, the one who has failed abysmally again and again can still be not only a disciple of the Lord, but one with him in his apostolic ministry. Peter assures us of this in the witness of his life and the teaching of his epistles.

Reflection on Saint Peter might also help us to look with greater compassion on the men who have been chosen to be the successors of the apostles, and even that man who has been chosen to be the successor of Saint Peter. There is a certain rightness in our expectation that men called to such a lofty service, to such a close identity with our Master, the Lord Jesus, should be men of exceptional life and perfection. And yet the fact remains that they too, like Peter and like each one of us, are poor, sinful human beings, each with his own weaknesses, his own struggles. Realizing this, we can see their limitations in perspective, and can support them with our loving and compassionate prayer and with a great deal of understanding. We will not expect too much from them, but we will hope for all things for them. For the same Risen Lord who transformed the weak, defensive braggart from the Sea of Galilee into the compassionate father of the whole Christian Church who was ready to show that love greater than which no man can show in the laying down of his life, can transform each of these shepherds until they are true images of the Good Shepherd.

Peter is a source of hope for us precisely because of his weaknesses and his failures. Through these he can give us not only hope—the hope that we too can overcome by that same grace of the Risen Christ—but also joy, as in the realization that our weaknesses and failures can be an instrument in God's hands to create in our hearts a deeper compassion. We can come to realize how it was that the great apostle Paul could glory in his infirmities. We can come to see how for those who love God, all things work together unto good—even our failures and our sins.

In order to facilitate further experience with Peter, I am including in this book an appendix in which I have listed the texts that speak about Simon Peter, as well as those that speak about the apostles and the disciples. When we desire to walk with Peter, we do not want simply to read these texts. First of all, we need to call upon the Spirit who inspired the author of the text, the same Spirit who dwells in the depths of our hearts, asking him to bring alive in us now the message of life that he desired to convey when he inspired the writer.

Then let us call upon Peter to intercede for us and be with us as we listen and seek to enter into his experience. We do not want so much to read these texts as to listen. We want to let the sacred writer, let the Spirit, let the Lord Jesus, our true Master, let Peter, our brother disciple, speak now to us with living words. At the end of such an encounter we want to be able to take a word or a phrase or a sentence and carry it with us as the epitome of the Word of Life that we have received. Then we can let our minds return to it again and again, letting it sink down into our hearts, forming them and creating in us that same attitude of discipleship that re-created Peter. This is true *lectio divina*—divine reading —in the sense it has always been understood in our Christian tradition. It is the kind of sacred reading that forms in us that mind which was in Christ Jesus, and makes us his disciples.

Through discipleship, Peter came to true freedom. He no longer needed the bravado of his younger years, the bravado that protected a false ego, for he came to know his own true dignity. He remained always a man of his own people and his own culture. In his public discourses and his epistles he again and again spoke out of the spirit and the letter of the Old Testament. Nevertheless, he came to know that in Christ Jesus we are "members of a chosen race, a royal priesthood, a people set apart" (1 Peter 2:9), that we are "slaves of no one except God" (1 Peter 2:16), that "no one can hurt us if we are determined to do only what is right. If we do have to suffer for being good we will count it a blessing. There is no need to be afraid or to worry. Simply reverence the Lord Christ in our hearts and always have an answer ready for those who ask us of the hope we all have" (1 Peter 3:13–15). In all this Peter had come clearly and joyfully to identify himself as the "servant and apostle of Jesus Christ" (2 Peter 1:1), a true disciple of the Divine Master.

Appendix

To facilitate our further walk with Peter in his discipleship, I am listing here the principal texts that speak of Peter, of the Apostles (or the Twelve), and of the Disciples.

Simon Peter—Cephas

The Call to Discipleship: Jn 1:35–51.
The Call to Ministry: Mt 4:18–22; Mk 1:16–20, 35–39; Lk 5:1–11.
The Call to Apostolic Leadership: Mt 10:1–42; Mk 3:13–19; Lk 6:12–16.
Mother-in-Law: Mt 8:14–15; Mk 1:29–31; Lk 4:38–39.
Jairus' Daughter: Mk 5:21–43; Mt 9:18–26; Lk 8:40–56.
Walking on the Waters: Mt 14:22–33; Mk 6:45–52; Jn 6:16–21.
Profession of Faith: Jn 6:67–71.
Peter Questions Jesus: Mt 15:15; 18:21–22; 19:27–30; Mk 10:28–31; 11:20–25; 13:3; Lk 12:35–48; 18:28–30.
Caesarea Philippi: Mt 16:13–23; Mk 8:27–33; Lk 9:18–22.
Transfiguration: Mt 17:1–13; Mk 9:2–8; Lk 9:28–36.
The Temple Tax: Mt 17:24–27.
Last Supper: Lk 22:7–13, 31–38; Jn 13:2–38; Mk 14:12–16.
Gethsemane: Mt 26:30–46; Mk 14:26–42; Lk 22:40–46; Jn 18:1–11.

Denial: Mt 26:57–75; Mk 14:53–72; Lk 22:54–62; Jn 18:15–27.

Resurrection: Mk 16:1–8; Mt 28:1–8; Lk 24:1–12, 33–35; Jn 20:1–10.

Restoration: Jn 21:1–23.

Election of Matthias: Acts 1:12–26.

Pentecost: Acts 2:1–41.

Cure of the Lame Man: Acts 3:1–4:22.

Ananias and Sapphira: Acts 5:1–11.

Confirmation Tour: Acts 8:14–17.

Cures: Acts 5:12–16; 9:32–35.

Cornelius: Acts 10:1–11:18.

Deliverance: Acts 12:1–19.

Council of Jerusalem: Acts 15:1–29.

Paul on Peter: Galatians 1:11–24; 2:1–14; 1 Cor 9:1–5; 15:3–8.

First and Second Epistles of Peter.

The Twelve Apostles

With Jesus: Mk 11:11; Lk 8:1.

Question Jesus: Mk 4:10–12.

Mission: Mk 6:7–13; Lk 9:1–6; Acts 2:42–43; 4:32–37; 5:12.

The Loaves and Fishes: Mk 6:30–44; Mt 14:13–21; 15:32–39; Lk 9:10–17; Jn 6:1–13.

Jealousy: Mt 20:24–28; Mk 9:33–37; Lk 9:46–48.

Increase Our Faith: Lk 17:5–6.

Prediction of the Passion: Mt 20:17–19; Mk 10:32–34; Lk 18:31–34.

Last Supper: Mk 14:17–21; Lk 22:14–18; Mt 26:17–25.

Resurrection: Lk 24:9–11.

Ascension: Acts 1:1–14.

Arrest: Acts 5:17–42.

Ordaining Deacons: Acts 6:1–6.

Courage: Acts 8:1.

Reward: Lk 22:28–30; Rev 18:20; 21:14.
Foundations of the Church: Ephesians 2:20–22.

Disciples

With Jesus: Mt 5:1; Mk 3:7–9; 4:34; 6:1; 8:14–21; 10:13–16, 46; 11:14; 12:41–44; 13:1; Lk 6:17–49; 7:11–17; 8:22–25; Jn 3:22; 4:27–38; 11:54.

Questioning Jesus: Mt 13:10–17, 36–43; 17:19–20; 18:1–4; 23:3–44; Mk 10:10; Lk 8:9–10; Jn 9:2; 16:17–19.

Conditions for Discipleship: Mt 8:18–22; 16:24–28; Mk 8:34–38; 10:23–27; Lk 12:22–32; Jn 8:31–32; 13:35; 15:1–8.

True Kinsmen: Mt 12:46–50.

A New Law: Mt 12:1–8; 15:1–14; Mk 7:1–23; Lk 6:1–5.

Prayer: Lk 11:1–13.

Fasting: Mk 2:18–22.

Mission: Lk 10:1–24.

Healing Ministry: Mk 9:14–29; Lk 9:37–43; Mt 17:14–20.

Children: Mt 19:13–15; Mk 10:17–22; Lk 18:15–17.

Sinners: Mk 2:15–17, 23–28; Mt 9:10–13; 12:1–8; Lk 5:29–32; 6:1–5.

Cana: Jn 2:1–11.

Calming the Storm: Mt 18:23–27; Mk 4:35–41; Lk 8:22–25.

Canaanite Woman: Mt 15:21–28.

Raising of Lazarus: Jn 11:1–44.

Anointing of Jesus: Mt 26:6–13; Mk 14:3–9; Jn 12:1–8.

Palm Sunday: Mt 21:1–11; Mk 11:1–11; Lk 19:28–40; Jn 12:12–19.

Eucharist: Mt 26:26–29; Mk 14:22–25; Lk 22:19–20; 1 Cor 11:23–25.

Resurrection: Jn 20:19–23.

Persecution: Acts 9:1–2.

Christians: Acts 11:26.